PRAISE FOR *5-D LEADERSHIP*

"This isn't just 'one more book' on leadership effectiveness. It offers a cohesive framework that includes many leadership styles and shows how to use the strengths you already have to select and apply the right style for your specific context. Powerful and practical."
> —*Brian J. Robertson, President & CEO, Ternary Software, Inc.*

"*5-D Leadership* is built around a unique model of leadership effectiveness that takes seriously the complexities of today's business world. It provides practical, workable tools and insightful suggestions for implementing its ideas. A truly important book."
> —*Roger L. Gilbertson, MD, President/CEO, Meritcare Health System*

"If, like Giulani, you are the perfect leader for a crisis but the wrong one at all other times; or if, like former President Jimmy Carter, you have only one trick in your bag and it's inadequate in many circumstances, read on—this book is for you. Like the great adventurer Shackleton, you will harness your leadership strengths."
> —*Andre LeBel, CEO, SOCAN*

5-D LEADERSHIP

5-D

LEADERSHIP

KEY DIMENSIONS
FOR LEADING IN THE REAL WORLD

SCOTT CAMPBELL & ELLEN SAMIEC

Davies-Black Publishing
Mountain View, California

Published by Davies-Black Publishing, a division of CPP, Inc., 1055 Joaquin Road, Mountain View, CA 94043; 800-624-1765.

Special discounts on bulk quantities of Davies-Black books are available to corporations, professional associations, and other organizations. For details, contact the Director of Marketing and Sales at Davies-Black Publishing: 650-691-9123; fax 650-623-9271.

Visit the Davies-Black Publishing Web site at www.daviesblack.com.

09 08 07 06 05   10 9 8 7 6 5 4 3 2 1
Printed in the United States of America

Library of Congress Cataloging-in-Publication Data
Campbell, Scott
    5-D leadership : key dimensions for leading in the real world / Scott Campbell & Ellen Samiec.
       p. cm.
    Includes bibliographical references and index.
    ISBN 0-89106-197-5 (hardcover)
       1. Leadership. I. Title: Five-D leadership. II. Samiec, Ellen. III. Title.
    HD57.7.C363 2005
    658.4'092--dc22

                                       2005021250
FIRST EDITION
First printing 2005

CONTENTS

Preface   ix

Acknowledgments   xi

1 Have We Been Misled?
Leadership Beyond Crisis   1

PART 1: UNDERSTANDING LEADERSHIP EFFECTIVENESS   21

2 When All You Have Is a Hammer . . .
The Five Leadership Dimensions   23

3 Some Assembly Required
How to Build a Leadership Dimension   45

4 When You're a Few Blocks Short
The Archimedes Principle   75

PART 2: KNOWING YOURSELF INSIDE OUT   89

5 Discover Your Leadership Strengths
Tools for Self-Awareness   91

6 Identify Your Leadership Dimensions
Tools for Self-Discovery   119

PART 3: IDENTIFYING CONTEXTUAL DYNAMICS   141

7 What Color Are Your Glasses?
Perception Isn't Always Reality   143

8 How Do You Gain 20/20 Vision?
Seeing Your Context Clearly   161

PART 4: LEVERAGING YOUR LEADERSHIP STRENGTHS   191

9 **Making a Good Thing Better**
    Maximizing an Already Good Fit   193

10 **You Don't Have to Take a Flying Leap**
    Bridging a Large Gap   205

    Epilogue   223

    Appendix A
    The Prevalence of Command and Control   227

    Appendix B
    Contrasting Management and Leadership   229

    Appendix C
    Four Recommended Formal Assessment Tools   231

    Notes   237
    About the Authors   243
    Index   245

PREFACE

Leadership is a hot commodity these days.

The 9/11 attacks, war, and economic malaise have highlighted the crucial role of effective leadership. Media coverage of the self-inflicted meltdown of organizations like Enron and Worldcom has focused our attention on the disastrous results of unethical and ineffective leadership. Even a casual review of current business books and magazines will reveal an astonishing number devoted to this important issue.

Leadership is also big business. North American organizations collectively spend millions of dollars on leadership development programs every year. MBA degree programs continue to flourish. Leadership coaching is a new and rapidly growing industry. Thousands of individuals are currently operating as registered leadership development coaches, and thousands more operate without affiliation to formal coaching organizations.

With so much time, attention, and money being spent on leadership development, you would think today's business leaders would exemplify the best in leadership effectiveness.

But such is not the case. Several recent surveys of medium and large organizations have demonstrated the existence of a widespread vacuum of leadership effectiveness in all sectors: private, public, and nonprofit.

What's going on?

There are two primary causes of this lack of effective leadership: The first is a widespread misunderstanding of the nature of leadership. The second is a serious deficit in the methodology of leadership development as it is commonly practiced today.

This book addresses both problems, and provides much-needed practical solutions.

The opening chapter confronts the misguided belief among a surprising number of business executives that there is a single best approach to leadership, applicable in all situations. Using three case studies, we show the dangers of this belief and contrast it with the truth that leadership effectiveness requires a continual shifting among a variety of leadership approaches.

The four parts of the book are designed to help you learn to match your leadership approach to your current context. Part 1 presents a new, real-world model of leadership effectiveness, describing in depth five leadership approaches—what we refer to as Leadership Dimensions— that are needed to master the complex business situations leaders face today. Most important, it introduces leaders—and aspiring leaders—to a practical method of leveraging *the strengths they already possess* in employing all five of these Leadership Dimensions.

Part 2 begins to apply the 5-D Leadership model by providing step-by-step processes for deepening your self-awareness in two critical areas: (1) your unique array of natural leadership strengths, and (2) the Leadership Dimensions that are most natural to you.

Part 3 then enables you to identify your current leadership context and determine which Leadership Dimensions are most appropriate in your business environment. You will begin by exploring two key challenges leaders experience in seeing their context clearly. The next focus is on seven common business contexts leaders encounter, with the most appropriate mix of Leadership Dimensions for each, and a process for determining which ones apply to you.

Finally, Part 4 consolidates the insights you have gained and outlines practical strategies for employing the Leadership Dimensions your context requires. When you learn how to improve an already good fit between your natural strengths and the Dimensions required by your context, you will turn to the challenge of overcoming any gaps between your strengths and the Leadership Dimensions you need to use.

Throughout the book, the emphasis is on learning to use the strengths you already have, rather than focusing on overcoming your weaknesses. This is far more effective, much faster, and definitely more enjoyable than traditional leadership development.

So, let's begin the journey by exploring—and exploding—the myth of one-size-fits-all leadership.

ACKNOWLEDGMENTS

While our names are on the cover of the book, the reality is that numerous individuals were involved in the realization of this project. This is our chance to thank them publicly. There are no words to adequately express the depth of our appreciation for and gratitude to these people, but we do want to acknowledge the part each of them played in helping us create this book.

Debbie Ellis offered unfailing encouragement and enthusiasm as a friend, and incalculable hours of time in reading the manuscript in its several iterations, providing keen editorial and linguistic insight along the way. Her influence in these pages is enormous.

Ellen Samiec gives special thanks to her husband, Bernie Schmidt, who provided loving support and encouragement, consistently conveying his belief in the value of the project and our ability to realize it. His strategic insight into key portions of the manuscript significantly enhanced the final product.

Carole Cameron offered not only her own story for inclusion in the book but also constant interest and encouragement.

Robert Allen and his colleague, Denise Michaels, provided critical information and wisdom in the process of turning a fledgling idea into a published book. Their expertise in the processes of creating a winning proposal, finding a publisher, writing the manuscript, and marketing the final product was invaluable.

William Brown, our literary agent, provided sage advice and handled superbly the discussions with our publisher.

The Davies-Black team was a delight to work with throughout the life of the project. Connie Kallback, Senior Acquisitions Editor, championed the project and provided insightful advice in its early phases. Jill Anderson-Wilson, Managing Editor, and her team utilized their editorial and copywriting skills to sharpen the text and create its professional look. Laura Simonds, Director of Marketing and Sales, provided energy, enthusiasm, wit, and insight in launching this enterprise into the world. Our thanks to all of them and the entire Davies-Black team.

Numerous friends, family members, and clients have demonstrated their interest, support, and encouragement along the way. All of them are appreciated.

Finally, thanks to the staff at the Coffee Tree Roastery, our unofficial "headquarters" for the project. The coffee, food, and ambiance combined to provide an ideal setting for many hours of brainstorming, discussion, and writing.

Authors' Note: Stories concerning our clients are true, but, unless permission was granted, their names and company identities have been changed or hidden in order to protect their anonymity. At times, some of the details were altered in order to ensure privacy.

CHAPTER 1

HAVE WE BEEN MISLED?
LEADERSHIP BEYOND CRISIS

Fit no stereotypes. Don't chase the latest management fads.
The situation dictates which approach best accomplishes
the team's mission.

—Colin Powell, former secretary of state

Who is *your* idea of an exceptionally effective leader? Rudy Giuliani? A good choice, given his remarkable response to the tragedy and challenges of 9/11. Jack Welch? He certainly worked magic at GE in the 1990s. Maybe you would choose Lou Gerstner Jr. for implementing the successful turnaround of the IBM juggernaut. All three men have written best-sellers recounting their exploits, successes, and philosophies of leadership. They have been lionized by the media, been featured in countless articles and interviews, and received abundant praise and recognition for their leadership effectiveness in immensely difficult circumstances.

The perception of these three leaders as heroes exemplifies a broader trend in the business world and the media. Outstanding leaders are often portrayed as individuals who have risen heroically to the challenges of extreme crisis situations. Lessons from leaders like Alexander the Great,

Winston Churchill, Abraham Lincoln, George W. Bush, Colin Powell, and Dwight D. Eisenhower are all part of this trend. People love a good story filled with drama, obstacles, and triumph. Larger-than-life crisis conquerors fit that mold.

While this makes for fascinating reading (and short-term inspiration), it offers little real help to leaders looking for answers to real problems. In fact, stories like these are misleading for two reasons: first, they ignore the fact that most business leaders do not operate in an environment of extreme crisis; and second, some of these heroes had very unheroic moments.

In an interview with *Newsweek* magazine, James O'Toole, research professor at the Center for Effective Organizations of the University of Southern California's Marshall School of Business and author of numerous books on leadership, discusses a story he read about Rudy Giuliani:

> The point [of the story] was: what the world needs now is leaders, not managers, that business leaders ought to look at Giuliani for the kind of forceful leadership we need. I think that's wrong on many scores. ***Most American businesses are not in a time of crisis.*** There were just a handful of companies affected directly by the World Trade Center attacks. To portray the general business culture as being in a crisis similar to what New York City is going through both underestimates the true kind of trauma and tragedy that happened in New York and grossly overstates the problems in corporations. (emphasis ours)[1]

Epic tales of leaders as heroic crisis managers don't describe the day-to-day reality of most leaders, and they ignore the fact that these same leaders were often floundering prior to the crisis or failed as leaders once the crisis passed. What is highly appropriate leadership in the face of crisis is typically ineffective and even destructive in other contexts. Winston Churchill is a vivid example of this phenomenon. Although brilliant as a forceful leader during World War II, he floundered in a time of peace because he did not adapt his authoritarian approach to the new reality.

It's not surprising that individuals trying to improve their power to lead sometimes look for a magic bullet, a single leadership approach guaranteed to work in all situations. They read about servant leadership, strategic leadership, visionary leadership, the *leader-as-coach,* or the *leader-as-commander* and focus on the one approach to leadership with which they're comfortable.

The belief that successful leaders operate in the same way in all circumstances is just not true. In fact, rigidity in one's leadership approach is a fast way to become yesterday's leader.

Take a look at three very different leaders: Rudy Giuliani, an instant icon with the perfect style for one indelible moment; President Jimmy Carter, whose inappropriate crisis management wildly missed the mark; and Sir Earnest Shackleton, whose flexible, adaptive leadership style actually saved the lives of his team.

THE GIULIANI MOMENT
9/11 and the Remaking of a Leader

Tomorrow New York is going to be here. And we're going to rebuild, and we're going to be stronger than we were before. . . . I want the people of New York to be an example to the rest of the country, and the rest of the world, that terrorism can't stop us.

— *Rudy Giuliani, September 11, 2001*

For having more faith in us than we had in ourselves, for being brave when required and rude where appropriate and tender without being trite, for not sleeping and not quitting and not shrinking from the pain all around him, Rudy Giuliani, Mayor of the World, is TIME's 2001 Person of the Year.

— *Nancy Gibbs, Time, December 31, 2001*

On the cover of *Time*, Giuliani's qualifications for the award were summarized in this simple phrase: "Tower of Strength." A fitting tribute. Giuliani's response to the tragedy and trauma of the horrendous events and aftermath of September 11, 2001, was remarkable and exactly what the city and the nation needed. With the president being kept out of sight for national security reasons during most of that day, Giuliani's presence and voice gave immediate comfort and inspiration not only to New Yorkers but also to the rest of the nation. His tireless efforts, demonstrations of courage and compassion, and words of inspiration and consolation continued to sustain us in the weeks that followed.

Given Giuliani's effectiveness in the aftermath of 9/11 it's easy to forget that just prior to that infamous day his reputation and approval rating were at their lowest ebb since he had become mayor. Such lack of public support contrasted starkly with the results of his 1997 reelection, when he garnered 57 percent of the popular vote, carrying four of New York City's five boroughs. What was it that got him elected initially in 1993 and reelected in 1997? And why was his popularity waning toward the end of his second term prior to the terrorist attacks?

Giuliani's past successes were patterned on confronting difficult situations with a firm hand. In the 1980s, as a U.S. Attorney in New York, Giuliani racked up an impressive number of convictions against Mafia bosses, drug dealers, white collar inside traders, and corrupt politicians. His reputation as a tough prosecutor was well earned. When he ran for mayor in 1993, the time seemed right in the eyes of most New Yorkers for such a tough, confrontational, authoritarian approach to running the city. Taxes and unemployment had risen through the ceiling; violent crime and drug abuse seemed to control whole segments of the city; tourist dollars were fleeing; and one out of seven New Yorkers was on welfare. Fear and pessimism were pervasive. It felt to many that the city was out of control.

Giuliani didn't disappoint those who were looking for a warrior to fight their battles and restore peace, order, and prosperity to the streets of New York. *Time* magazine recorded Giuliani's perspective on his election mandate: "People didn't elect me to be a conciliator. . . . They wanted somebody who was going to change this place. How do you expect me to change it if I don't fight with somebody? You don't change ingrained human behavior without confrontation, turmoil, anger."[2]

A radical crackdown on crime, a stringently enforced welfare-to-work program, and strong tax reform measures marked his first term and seemed to deliver the promised results. Serious crime was reduced by more than a third and murders by almost half within two years of his election. Welfare rolls were cut in half. Taxes were cut by $2.5 billion. Redevelopment proceeded at a remarkable pace. Prosperity returned and tourism dollars rose to unprecedented levels.

So it was little surprise when Giuliani handily won a second term. But things didn't stay rosy for Rudy. By September 2001, Giuliani's approval rating had dropped to below 40 percent. Now that New York's crime crisis had passed, people grew weary of Giuliani's constant battling with political opponents, his own appointees, the media, jaywalkers, street vendors, and even his own wife. His successes through his hard-line approach had parallel failures in areas where a more conciliatory, collaborative style may have served better (educational reform and relations with visible minority groups being two such examples). In March 1999, an instinctive desire to defend the police—and perhaps his policy of being tough on crime—led him to release the juvenile crime record of Patrick Dorismond, an unarmed security guard shot to death by undercover officers with whom he struggled. Giuliani wanted to demonstrate Dorismond's propensity for violence, declaring that the dead waive their rights to privacy and that Dorismond was "no altar boy." In blaming the victim, he appalled the city.

The combination of Giuliani's inability (or unwillingness) to adapt his leadership approach and his very public marital problems seemed to guarantee that his reputation would be very mixed in the minds of most New Yorkers when his second term expired. Had he been eligible to run for a third term, and had the election been held on September 10, 2001, Giuliani would almost certainly have been looking for another job the next day.

September 11 changed all that. That cataclysmic event remade him into a leader of almost mythic proportions. It was the *Giuliani Moment*.

Giuliani's immediate responses to the destruction, chaos, terror, and sorrow of that day were truly remarkable. His efficiency, aura of authority, rapid decision making, inspirational words, and compassionate actions toward the victims and their families fit perfectly the needs and demands of the moment. His ongoing actions in the days and weeks that followed were likewise exemplary. Giuliani tirelessly attended funerals of victims, spoke eloquently at special events and press conferences, visited with and encouraged laborers, firefighters, police officers, and relief workers at Ground Zero, toured the site with visiting dignitaries, and prodded businesses and the stock exchange to get on with business and not let the terrorists win. These decisive actions were critical in helping the city begin to recover from the events of September 11.

His masterful response to 9/11 should not obscure the fact that his leadership style was not widely appreciated just before that infamous day. This is the *Giuliani Moment: A new set of circumstances launches a faltering leader into renewed effectiveness when his or her singular leadership approach happens to match the needs of the moment.*

Unless you are gifted at repeatedly finding situations and environments that call for a certain approach—or are fortunate enough to have those situations repeatedly find you—overreliance on one Dimension of leadership is usually a recipe for lost effectiveness. Continuing to employ your past leadership style when the context has changed can ruin you. Jimmy Carter's presidency poignantly illustrates the point.

THE CARTER DISCONNECT
Energy, Hostages, and the Unmaking of a Leader

Few stories better illustrate the intersection of character and leadership than the story of Jimmy Carter. The very qualities that got him elected—tenacity, religious certitude and an absolute confidence in his abilities—made it nearly impossible for him to govern.

—Adriana Bosch, writer and director, Wisconsin Public Television

In January 1975, when he began his campaign to become the Democratic presidential candidate, Jimmy Carter was virtually unknown to the American public. He was a long shot to win his own party's nomination, let alone the presidential election. Nevertheless, two years later Carter was inaugurated as the thirty-ninth president of the United States.

Three factors merged to lift Carter from national obscurity to the presidency:

- Changes to the rules for candidates

- Carter's campaign style and emphasis

- Public disaffection with politicians

The first factor involved extensive changes made to the rules for party and presidential campaigns in the early 1970s. Carter was fortunate to have two assets that allowed him to capitalize on these changes. One was an early start to full-time campaigning. His governorship of Georgia had ended in 1974, allowing him to devote himself full-time to the campaign process at a very early stage (Carter formally entered the race on December 12, 1974). The other was a very shrewd campaign strategy, largely devised by a young aide named Hamilton Jordan.

The second factor in Carter's success was his campaign style and focus. Carter understood the loss of respect and trust in political leadership that many Americans experienced after the Vietnam War and Watergate. He promised he would never lie to the American people, underscoring that promise in these opening statements in his 1976 presidential campaign brochure:

> Our whole system depends on trust. The only way that I know to be trusted is to be trustworthy. To be open, direct and honest. It's as simple as that.[3]

This uplifting theme fit well the climate of the early post-Vietnam, post-Watergate era. So did Carter's religious and ethical beliefs. Rather than alienating the public, Carter's unabashed declaration of his religious faith and moral perspectives seemed to assure people that he would act decently, sincerely, and morally. Carter's religious orientation was not a pretense. It was the core of his being and profoundly influenced his actions and decisions. As Fred Greenstein says, "Carter stands alone among the modern presidents in the centrality of religious principles to his political leadership, and, indeed, his very being."[4]

The third factor in Carter's electoral victory was his positioning of himself as an outsider to the Washington political apparatus. And an outsider he was. Carter's political experience was entirely at the state level in Georgia—two terms in the state senate and one term as governor. One might have expected voters to view this as the rather limited experience of an obscure southerner. Instead, many hoped his outsider status might lead to refreshing change in the now-disgraced political machinations of Washington.

And so Jimmy Carter became the next American president.

In the first few months of his presidency Carter enjoyed great public support. One month after his inauguration, Gallup pollsters reported an approval rating of 66 percent. By mid-March it had climbed to 75 percent. This support, however, soon began to erode. Just one year later only 34 percent of Americans were pleased with his leadership. In his final year as president, Carter received the lowest-ever presidential approval rating (even worse than the disgraced Richard Nixon's). Carter's support had slumped to a mere 21 percent.

What happened? The answer, quite simply, is that Carter continued to lead as a president in the same way he had as a governor. Five elements were particularly evident in Carter's leadership approach as governor of Georgia.

The first was the centrality of his ethics. This was evident in his gubernatorial inaugural address, when he declared, "The time for racial discrimination is over. . . . No poor, rural, weak, or black person should ever have to bear the additional burden of being deprived of the opportunity for an education, a job or simple justice."

A second element was his bulldoglike tenacity. This was demonstrated when he pushed through a sweeping governmental reorganization plan, the centerpiece of his legislative program.

The third component of his leadership style was his acute self-reliance and self-confidence. Even though Carter surrounded himself with loyal, dedicated staff, he characteristically operated as a loner. He spent vast amounts of time ingesting documents and mastering the minute details of situations and options, believing that he was the best one to handle many situations.

Carter's preference for face-to-face persuasion constituted a fourth aspect of his leadership approach. Carter believed that if he could sit down with someone in person, his calm demeanor, intelligence, and sincerity would achieve the results he wanted. Customarily it worked.

The fifth element of his leadership modus operandi was a populist tactic of appealing directly to the public to gain support for his initiatives. Carter disdained the machinery of government and often sidestepped the political norm of building consensus and lobbying other politicians for support on different initiatives. He preferred to use public pressure as a means of swaying votes in the Georgia senate.

An inflexible adherence to these same leadership tactics, successful in the relatively tranquil context of Georgia politics, ultimately led to Carter's unmaking as the leader of the nation. The realities of Washingtonian politics and the emergence of major domestic and international crises required leadership responses very different from those that Carter had employed thus far in his career. His dependence on a singular Leadership Dimension led to several failed initiatives and a public perception of ineffectiveness. This is the *Carter Disconnect.*

Carter's loner approach cost him the support of his team and the Democratic Party. His attempts to personally master the myriad details of circumstances and issues rather than rely on his staff were cumbersome, time-consuming, and disaffecting to his team. They also cost him party support. At times Carter would garner Democratic support for an initiative, only to drop the proposal without warning or explanation, having alone decided not to pursue it.

Furthermore, Washington politics required compromise—something Carter usually loathed, equating compromise with a betrayal of his ethics. According to Douglas Brinkley, director of the Eisenhower Center for American Studies at Metropolitan College of the University of New Orleans, this unwillingness to compromise and his naiveté regarding the need to play the Washington political game resulted in Carter alienating both the liberal and the more conservative wings of the Democratic party. Thus even with substantial Democratic majorities in both the Senate and the House, many of Carter's initiatives were either rejected or significantly watered down (particularly his flagship energy bill). Ted Kennedy's strong challenge to an incumbent president for the party's presidential nomination in 1979 was an indicator of how much Carter's style had disaffected his own party. The unyielding approach that had worked at the state level had little success on the national scene.

This is not to say that Carter attained no political achievements using his typical leadership approach. His tenacity worked well in pushing through the Panama Canal treaty and with the Camp David peace accord. Carter's ability to persuade people individually also played a key role in brokering and salvaging the peace accord reached between Egyptian president Anwar el-Sadat and Israeli prime minster Menachem

Begin. But generally, Carter's failure to adapt his leadership approach to the new realities of national politics and the way Washington worked cost him crucial support. With his failure to get several key programs passed into law (for example, national health insurance, welfare reform, and controls on hospital costs), he began to lose public support and gained a reputation for being powerless.

Carter's loss of public esteem was reinforced by his responses to three major crises that occurred during his presidency. During the Carter years, the U.S. economy "tanked." Inflation, interest rates, and unemployment all climbed steadily during his term. The deficit continued to balloon, and the value of the U.S. dollar eroded greatly. And then the energy crisis occurred. Shortages of oil and gasoline in early July 1979 led to trucker blockades of expressways. Rioting took place in several cities. On July 15, Carter responded to the crisis with a televised address in which he focused on what he referred to as a widespread "crisis of confidence" in the nation rather than on specific solutions to the economic and energy crises.

Quickly dubbing Carter's address "the malaise speech," commentators and the public alike felt Carter blamed the American public rather than providing effective leadership. As historian Roger Wilkins says, "When your leadership is demonstrably weaker than it should be, you don't then point at the people and say, 'It's your problem.' If you want the people to move, you move them the way Roosevelt moved them, or you exhort them the way Kennedy or Johnson exhorted them. You don't say, 'It's your fault.'"[5] Carter's address lacked both vision and inspiration, crucial ingredients for leadership in a time of crisis.

The other crisis, which perhaps damaged Carter most, was the taking of more than sixty U.S. American hostages from the American embassy in Tehran on November 4, 1979. Carter had granted the deposed shah of Iran entry to the United States on humanitarian grounds for treatment of his cancer, despite concerns that there might be reprisals. This exacerbated the ongoing frustration of the Iranian people with the United States. A group of Iranian university students retaliated by storming the American embassy and seizing its members.

Carter felt that the safe return of all the hostages was his personal responsibility and clearly made their freedom his number one priority.

His religious beliefs, including a strong aversion to any loss of life what-soever, played a strong role in his mission. The depth of this conviction was evident during a meeting with the National Security Council and Pentagon heads concerning a planned rescue attempt. Carter asked if U.S. soldiers could use rubber bullets so that no Iranian guards would be killed.[6] This concern for human life was laudable, but not necessarily the most appropriate political or military response in a hostile situation.

As is common in such circumstances, public support rallied for Carter in the initial months of the crisis, surging from 32 percent in November to 56 percent in January. But as winter turned to spring and patient negotiations didn't bring the hostages home, the public began to demand stronger action. By April, public support had once again dropped, registering only 39 percent.

On April 11, 1979, Carter approved a high-risk rescue operation, called Desert One. An unfortunate series of mechanical failures and weather conditions forced him to abort the mission, but not before eight servicemen were killed in an accident. The next day, Iranian television showed footage of the smoking remains of the U.S. rescue attempt. Americans watched in dismay, and many blamed Carter's weak leadership for the botched attempt, the loss of life, and America's seeming impotence.

The crisis lasted a total of 444 days, ending on the very day Carter turned over presidential power to his successor, Ronald Reagan. Carter's inability to return the hostages was a key factor in his electoral loss—especially when contrasted with Reagan's stringent campaign rhetoric accusing Carter of appeasing Iran and claiming that he would never negotiate with terrorists.

Jimmy Carter's very public demise as a leader is regularly replicated on a much smaller and usually much less visible scale in the business world. *The Carter Disconnect occurs when a leader continues to rely on one Dimension of leadership even though it is inappropriate in the current context. This inevitably leads to the collapse of leadership effectiveness.* The business equivalents to losing the presidential election are being fired, staff turnover, and lower profits.

Our survey of leadership effectiveness so far has shown us two common phenomena. Giuliani's story demonstrates the fortuitous recovery of one's reputation when circumstances emerge that fit one's preferred leadership approach. Carter's story shows the negative consequences of the inability to change one's approach as required by the emergence of a new/different context. But there is another story to be told: a story that reveals the secret of enduring leadership effectiveness.

THE SHACKLETON SECRET
Matching Response to Context

After the conquest of the South Pole by Amundsen . . . there remained but one great main object of Antarctic journeyings—the crossing of the South Polar continent from sea to sea.

After long months of ceaseless anxiety and strain, after times when hope beat high and times when the outlook was black indeed, we have been compelled to abandon the ship, which is crushed beyond all hope of ever being righted, we are alive and well, and we have stores and equipment for the task that lies before us. The task is to reach land with all the members of the Expedition. It is hard to write what I feel.

—Sir Earnest Shackleton

The remarkable story of Sir Earnest Shackleton's harrowing *Endurance* expedition to the Antarctic (1914–16) has enjoyed renewed popularity in the past decade. It is a compelling story of courage, hardship, resourcefulness, and triumph over the forces of nature. Although Shackleton didn't achieve his primary objective—the crossing of the Antarctic on foot—he nevertheless demonstrated remarkable leadership throughout the expedition.

Shackleton's charismatic personality, optimistic nature, and previous polar experience all played a role in his effectiveness. But his real brilliance lay in his ability to employ a variety of leadership approaches in response to differing situations. Shackleton, unlike Giuliani or Carter, was able to draw upon a *range* of approaches and match them to the specific context. That is the *Shackleton Secret*.

Shackleton's leadership wisdom was demonstrated from the very start of the expedition. When interviewing a prospective group member (more than 5,000 men applied for the voyage!), he used unorthodox questions to try to discern their suitability. For example, Reginald James, the *Endurance* physicist, recalled his interview thus: "Shackleton asked me if my teeth were good, if I suffered from varicose veins, if my circulation was good, if I had a temper, and if I could sing. At this question, I probably looked a bit taken aback, for I remember he said, 'Oh, I don't mean any Caruso stuff; but I suppose you can shout a bit with the boys.'"[7]

Shackleton regularly asked the question about singing. It had become for him a standard test of a person's attitude toward teamwork. Based on his previous experience in polar exploration, Shackleton was convinced that a positive team atmosphere was nonnegotiable for success. He judged that certain personal attributes were needed beyond technical skills and did his best to ascertain that the person was a good fit. As he put it: "The men selected must be qualified for the work, and they must have the special qualifications required to meet polar conditions. They must be able to live together in harmony for a long period of time without outside communication, and it must be remembered that the men whose desires lead them to the untrodden paths of the world have generally marked individuality. It was no easy matter for me to select the staff."[8] This care in selecting men who were "team players" accounts for much of the relative peace and harmony that prevailed throughout the odyssey.

Having selected the full complement of twenty-six individuals, Shackleton began the voyage south from London on August 1, 1914. The *Endurance* sailed to Buenos Aires and then to the whaling station on South Georgia Island, a subantarctic island group in the South Atlantic. They arrived in early November.

On December 5, 1914, Shackleton and his group departed, planning to sail to Vahsel Bay, a distance of some 1,000 miles. The plan was to arrive at Vahsel Bay well in advance of winter (remember, we're talking about the *South* Pole) so the expedition party could disembark and the *Endurance* and her crew could return in time to winter at South Georgia Island. Shackleton had arranged to have the explorers picked up at the Beardmore Glacier on the west side of the Antarctic by another ship, the *Aurora*.

Unfortunately, Mother Nature did not cooperate with Shackleton's plan. By January 18, 1915, after maneuvering around and blasting through heavy pack ice for weeks, the *Endurance* was solidly frozen in a vast ice floe—only one day's sail from the intended landing site. Over the next few days, Shackleton and the crew could only watch as the current in the Weddell Sea began pulling the ice floe and their captive boat in a slow northwesterly direction, farther and farther from their desired location.

The short-term objective was to ride out their entrapment until the ice pack released the *Endurance* to sail again. Knowing the unpredictability of the polar region, Shackleton had stocked extensive supplies of food, coal, and warm clothing. A regular supply of seals provided fresh meat. So, although the likelihood of a successful mission was now remote, circumstances were not desperate.

Indeed, a point often overlooked in telling the story of the *Endurance* expedition is that the longest portion of the voyage was not a crisis situation, but rather an extended period of relative inactivity, fighting boredom and the pressure of living in such close quarters. This relatively mundane phase of the journey required a very different leadership response than that of the crisis conqueror.

Using a variety of tactics, Shackleton set about to prevent the boredom, conflict, and low morale that captivity could create. He first provided structure and appropriate work for everyone. A definite daily schedule and specific assignments gave the men a means to focus and use their energy in constructive ways. This was balanced by regular times of fun and recreation—from soccer games on the ice floe to sing-alongs and skit nights. His own occasional spontaneous antics (for example, waltzing with the captain) were matched with planned birthday celebrations and festive meals for special events. In all these ways and more, Shackleton sought to create a strong sense of togetherness.

Indeed, from the very beginning of the voyage, Shackleton had put an emphasis on creating unity aboard ship. Customarily, on such expeditions the officers, seamen, and scientists all kept to their own groups, reflecting the educational, occupational, and class distinctions of the day. Shackleton sought instead to democratize and unify the entire group. Scientists were required to share in the ship's chores, and crewmen helped take scientific readings and gather samples. Everyone had a turn at steering the ship and pulling night watch duty. This camaraderie proved critical in combating the long days of entrapment in the ice (it would also prove critical for the stressful period of prolonged crisis that was to come).

Shackleton also sought to develop and maintain strong personal relationships with all aboard (including, ultimately, a stowaway discovered shortly after leaving Buenos Aires). He took time to talk regularly with each of the men; even those who were "harder to like" received his attention. When one of the least popular crew members fell ill, Shackleton had him share his own cabin and personally attended to his recovery. This relational Dimension of Shackleton's leadership accounts in great part for the deep loyalty that he received throughout even the bleakest and most dangerous parts of the journey.

At the same time, when needed, Shackleton could also be stern, even confrontational. For example, in dealing with disruptive behavior from a crewman, Shackleton took immediate action: when a delegation of the seamen complained to him about bullying treatment at the hands of the bosun, John Vincent, Shackleton immediately summoned Vincent to his cabin. This large, swaggering trawlerhand left the cabin shaken, demoted, and rehabilitated! He caused no further specific problems. As First Officer Lionel Greenstreet put it, "He [Shackleton] could put on a look, a disdainful look that made you shrivel up. He could be very cutting when he wanted to, but I think it was more the look."[9] On a few other key occasions, Shackleton proved capable of dealing swiftly, directly, and commandingly with difficult individuals.

These examples of flexible leadership styles—applied to the changing needs of the crew and changing circumstances—demonstrate the Shackleton Secret in action: adapting one's leadership approach to the context.

Shackleton also proved to be a remarkable crisis conqueror, responding skillfully to unimaginably difficult circumstances. It is this aspect of his story for which he is most frequently remembered.

In the fall of 1915, having drifted northwest more than 750 miles since becoming icebound, the *Endurance* began to suffer critical damage from the pressure of the ice pack. On October 27, Shackleton was forced to order the men to abandon ship. The damage was beyond repair and it had become dangerous to stay on board. Salvaging the three lifeboats, the sleds and dogs, and the supplies, the men set up Ocean Camp on the ice floe. They were now 350 miles from the nearest land and the temperature was −15° Fahrenheit.

Shackleton immediately demonstrated his ability to respond effectively in a crisis. Gathering the men together, he explained their situation, reviewed the options, and then offered them a concrete plan of action. Shackleton thanked them for their efforts thus far and asked for their support. All the while his manner was calm, confident, and optimistic. Entries from two of the men's diaries show the immediate impact of this moment. R. W. James wrote:

> He spoke to us in a group, telling us that he intended to march the party across the [ice] to the west . . . that he thought we ought to manage five miles a day, and that if we all worked together it could be done. . . . I can't remember the matter being discussed in any way. We were in a mess, and the Boss was the man who could get us out. It is a measure of his leadership that this seemed almost axiomatic.

The meteorologist, Leonard Hussey, stated, "it was a characteristic speech—simple, moving, optimistic and highly effective. It brought us out of our doldrums, our spirits rose, and we had our supper."[10]

Next, Shackleton demonstrated his concern for his men in a most practical way. Only eighteen reindeer-skin sleeping bags were available, the remaining being wool and much less warm. Shackleton arranged for the drawing of straws, ostensibly so that the allocation of bags would be perceived as fair. Through some act of subterfuge, all the officers ended up with the wool bags, a fact not lost on the rest of the men. Able Seamen Bakewell noted, "There was some crooked work in the drawing as Sir Earnest, Mr. Wild . . . Captain Worsley and some of the other officers all drew wool bags. The fine warm fur bags all went to the men under them."[11]

After a failed attempt to walk to open water, the company had to settle down to wait for warmer weather and the breaking up of the pack ice. Shackleton continued to ensure a daily regimen, specific assignments, recreation, and entertainment. He also made sure that food rations were carefully determined and distributed. Emergency drills were held practicing a speedy departure. Shackleton left nothing to chance. All the while he continued to maintain an optimistic outlook with his men. Shackleton lived by his own belief that "optimism is true moral courage." This was much appreciated and frequently noted by his men. Over the next several months of camping they drew strength, comfort, and hope from his resolute confidence.

Over time, the situation steadily deteriorated. The number of penguins and seals used for fresh meat was dwindling, and as the pack ice continued its northern drift and temperatures rose, the ice began to break up, causing dangerous crevices and splits to suddenly appear.

However, the continuing drift now created the possibility of reaching several nearby islands, and on April 9, 1916, the three lifeboats were launched when a lane of water opened up. In the midst of heavy seas, gale-force winds, pack ice, and icebergs, the pursuit of land began. As Caroline Alexander states, "The men had been trapped in the ice for fifteen months. But their real ordeal had just begun."[12]

Over the next seven days Shackleton would forgo sleep, standing erect day and night on the stern counter of the lifeboat as a visible beacon of leadership. Several times he had to alter the intended destination and shift direction based on changing weather, wind, and ice conditions. He made sure the men got as much rest as was feasible, though conditions often made sleep impossible. Finally, against all odds, the lifeboats landed on Elephant Island, a deserted, bleak, and inhospitable mountain terrain. After having been at sea for more than sixteen months, upon disembarking many of the men "filled their pockets with stones, or rolled along the beach, burying their faces in the stones and pouring handfuls over them."[13]

Shackleton soon realized that the next step in their arduous journey home would be an attempt to cross the Southern Ocean, the most difficult and dangerous water in the world, and land on South Georgia Island. With many of his crew being too weak to hazard the journey, he chose a group of five men to accompany him in the *James Caird*, the largest of the three lifeboats. The remaining men were to be left behind on Elephant Island in the hope of eventual rescue, should the voyage of the *James Caird* succeed. On April 24, they set out to accomplish what all knew was highly improbable—sailing a lifeboat 800 miles in the midst of gale-force winds, snow, ice, and colossal waves, using only a sextant to navigate. The journey was an amazing display of courage, skill, and good fortune.

Miraculously, after seventeen days at sea, they reached land.

On May 10, Shackleton and his disheveled crew landed on the west side of South Georgia Island, the opposite side from where the whaling station was located. Weather and ocean conditions, as well as the severely depleted state of three of the five crew members, made an attempt to sail around the southern end of the island impossible. Instead, Shackleton chose the two men who were least exhausted to accompany him on a thirty-mile trek over the mountains, leaving the other three behind to await rescue. In spite of setbacks, fatigue, and severe weather, thirty-six hours later, the three men walked into the whaling station at Husvick. So unkempt were they that Shackleton reported scaring two children and an old man in the whaling station.

Shackleton immediately arranged for the rescue of the three men left behind on the other side of the island. Only three days later, though exhausted, he boarded a whaler for the first of three attempts to rescue the rest of the crew still camped back on Elephant Island. Although it would ultimately take four months before the rescue was achieved, when they finally arrived, Shackleton was overjoyed to find that all his men had survived. Thus ended one of the most amazing stories of survival and leadership effectiveness in the annals of history.

Throughout this journey Shackleton faced a wide range of circumstances: routine ship life, months of relative inactivity, weeks of anxious uncertainty, days of absolute crisis. In all these shifting contexts, he maintained an incredibly high degree of leadership effectiveness. What accounts for this? *Shackleton adapted his leadership approach and emphasis to the needs and demands of the particular context. That's the Shackleton Secret to leadership effectiveness.*

THE LEADERSHIP EDGE
Leveraging Your Strengths to Broaden Your Organizational Impact

Leadership is not the private reserve of a few charismatic men and women. It's a process ordinary people use when they're bringing forth the best from themselves and others. Liberate the leader in everyone, and extraordinary things happen.

—James M. Kouzes and Barry Z. Posner

Shackleton would have heartily endorsed Kouzes and Posner's perspective on leadership. It is another way of describing the Shackleton Secret. Effectiveness is based on reading the situation at hand and choosing an appropriate leadership response. This is in contrast to the more common practice (demonstrated differently by Giuliani and Carter) of depending on one approach in all situations.

The question is this: Is it just the notable few like Shackleton, unusually gifted, who have what it takes to be flexible in their leadership approaches? *Absolutely not.*

This book will show you a quick, easy way to increase your flexibility in order to maximize your leadership effectiveness. It's a revolutionary approach that draws on the strengths you already have.

This practical guide will give you the tools to identify and build on those strengths to increase your range of leadership approaches. You will see which approaches are needed for a variety of business contexts and how you can immediately use your strengths to start leading with the appropriate approach.

Some other practices in leadership development do help individuals identify their strengths, but their primary emphasis lies in identifying and overcoming a leader's *weaknesses.* This traditional approach is a waste of precious time and energy and, ultimately, it's self-defeating. It places your focus on what you lack instead of on the skills and talents you already possess. Focusing on weaknesses can lead to frequent failures in attempts at major change and usually yields minimal development.

The good news is you don't need a major personality overhaul to increase your range of Leadership Dimensions and your effectiveness. 5-D Leadership is faster and far less painful, and the results are often astonishing.

CONCLUSION

So, are you ready to begin the journey? You may not end up taking people to the ends of the earth like Sir Earnest, but you will maximize your impact on your world.

In the next chapter, we will explore the five leadership approaches needed for today's complex business world.

PART **1**

UNDERSTANDING LEADERSHIP EFFECTIVENESS

In Chapter 1 we challenged the common practice of depending on one leadership approach in all situations. Now, in this first section, we present our model of leadership effectiveness—matching your leadership approach to the context.

Chapter 2 outlines the five leadership approaches, or *Leadership Dimensions*, leaders need in order to respond to today's complex business world. Each Dimension is first defined and then illustrated with a real-world example. We then describe the strategic objectives each approach is designed to achieve.

Chapter 3 details the concrete actions—*Building Blocks*—required to employ each of the five Leadership Dimensions. Signs of the effective or ineffective use of these Building Blocks are provided.

Chapter 4 describes a practical means of capitalizing on the strengths you already possess in learning to employ all five Leadership Dimensions—an approach called *leveraging your strengths.*

WHEN ALL YOU HAVE IS A HAMMER...

THE FIVE LEADERSHIP DIMENSIONS

*Under pressure, companies tend to fall back
upon what they know, so they often end up trying
to solve problems with the same tools that got them
into trouble in the first place.*

—*Alan Cooper*

As a young husband I [Scott] wanted to impress my new bride with my home repair savvy. Unfortunately, I brought only one tool into the marriage: a hammer. I thought I could easily make do with other household items as substitutes for the real thing, and money was tight, so I resisted buying other tools for some time.

One day I was attempting to replace a light switch faceplate. The screws needed were standard slot-head screws, so I confidently concluded that an ordinary table knife would do just as well as a screwdriver.

Later that day, with a bandage firmly wrapped around the thumb of my left hand, I dropped in at my local hardware store and bought my first-ever 6-in-1 screwdriver.

HOME REPAIRS FROM HELL
When the Tool Doesn't Match the Task

When all you have is a hammer, everything looks like a nail.

—*Anonymous*

The thumb incident serves as an example of more than severe mechanical ineptitude. It highlights an important truth: using the wrong tool for the job is more than just ineffective; it's potentially dangerous. You can inflict a lot of damage when you don't use the right tool.

This isn't just a truth about home repairs. It's the definitive truth for leaders. Many executives and managers are disappointed and confused by the lack of morale, initiative, creativity, or commitment demonstrated by their staff members. High turnover rates, lack of loyalty to the company, and marginal concern for the customer add to management's frustration. Many of these same executives fail to see any connection between such staff dynamics and their leadership approach. In reality, these dynamics are often the manifestation of the damage caused by a leadership style that is inappropriate to the context. Effective leadership requires using the right tool—or approach—for the right situation.

WHAT IS EFFECTIVE LEADERSHIP ANYWAY?
A Definition That Works

Effective leadership is the process of achieving desired results through people's willing participation.[1]

—*Scott Campbell and Ellen Samiec*

The heart of this definition is the phrase "through people's willing participation." Assuredly, leadership is about achieving results. It will not suffice to create a warm, happy workplace that goes bankrupt! Good leaders are results oriented. But great leaders know that the best and most sustainable results are achieved through people who are fully engaged in their work.

Truly effective leaders inspire and draw forth wholehearted involvement and commitment to the desired results from their followers. Drawing forth that commitment will require a variety of approaches. For example, in a crisis situation where people are afraid, nervous, or confused, a Commanding approach gives followers confidence in their leader, fostering commitment. In those circumstances, people respond to a strong, decisive leader. When not in crisis, most workers want to focus on more than just survival. Nonetheless, they long to give themselves to something worthy of their best efforts. This is what makes Visioning leadership such a powerful tool. Or consider your top performers: Their desire to grow and develop through increased opportunities, rather than stagnate and grow bored in their current role, makes Coaching a key response in sustaining their willing participation.

> *Leadership is a relationship between those who aspire to lead and those who choose to follow.*
> —James M. Kouzes and Barry Z. Posner

It takes all these approaches—and more—to earn willing participation from your people. No one approach alone can do this. It is the willing participation and commitment of your people that separates adequate performance from outstanding performance—and great companies from the merely good.

THE FULL TOOLKIT
The Five Leadership Dimensions and What Each Does Well

> *What has become clear over the years is that a "best" leadership style does not exist; rather a successful leader is one that matches the style with the current situation to maximize productivity and human satisfaction. The adaptability of a leader appears to be his or her greatest asset.*
>
> —Anne Breen

We have found that a fully equipped leadership toolkit includes five specific tools, or approaches. Together, these leadership tools enable a leader

to respond effectively to the changing contexts and situations they encounter.

We refer to these approaches as *Leadership
Dimensions.* In the same way that three spatial
dimensions (height, width, and length) are needed to
fully describe an object, five Leadership Dimensions are
needed to describe an effective leader. These five Dimensions
constitute the fully equipped toolkit for today's business leader.

Each Leadership Dimension involves distinct *objectives* and *tactics.*
Understanding the objectives unique to each Dimension is critical for
determining which Dimension to use in a particular situation. The tactics describe specific actions a leader must take to accomplish that
Dimension's objectives.

What follows is an overview of the objectives of each of the five
Dimensions. In the next chapter we will explore the core tactics of each
Dimension.

DIMENSION 1: COMMANDING
Taking Charge

The only safe ship in a storm is leadership.
—Faye Wattleton, Center for Gender Equality

Commanding is *taking charge and seeking immediate compliance to quickly effect a desired result.* In specific situations, it is an invaluable tool in the toolkit.

Commanding for a Harley-Davidson Turnaround

In 2003 Harley-Davidson celebrated its one hundredth
anniversary. The Harley name carries with it tremendous
brand recognition, conjuring up images of *Easy Rider,* freedom, and
independence. The company is the current North American market
leader in heavyweight motorcycles and runs a close second to Honda for
overall market share. It is widely recognized as one of the best-managed

and most profitable companies in the country. Its current success over-shadows the crisis the company experienced in the early 1980s. In 1969, Harley had been purchased by American Machine and Foundry (AMF). In the face of strong Japanese competition, the Harley-Davidson division market shares declined steadily throughout the 1970s. In 1980, for the first time in fifty years, Harley-Davidson lost money. It was on the road to bankruptcy. Public perception was so negative that despite a powerful brand image and an aggressive marketing campaign, when the division was put up for sale there were no interested buyers!

Traditional command-and-control leadership saved the company in the early 1980s and restored it to profitability and market dominance. In 1981 thirteen members of the Harley-Davidson management team purchased the company from AMF in a leveraged buyout. Richard Teerlink was hired in 1981 as CFO, becoming president and CEO in 1987. In reflecting on the kind of leadership it took to stop the hemorrhaging and restore prosperity, Teerlink asserts,

> We believe that traditional command and control hierarchies are of limited effectiveness and have a host of fatal flaws in the long run. But command and control works in certain situations—and in fact may be the only thing that works when circumstances are desperate enough. If an organization is under extreme pressure—so much so that one wrong move can mean the death of an organization—then an authoritarian system of controls may be absolutely necessary.[2]

Vaughan Beals, CEO from 1981 to 1987, piloted the turnaround. Beals demonstrated a highly skilled use of the Commanding Dimension of leadership in engineering Harley-Davidson's return to prominence. But the undertaking involved many difficult and painful decisions. Harley moved to cut costs by slashing its workforce by 40 percent. Senior management had shown union leaders the financials and they reluctantly agreed that the move was justified. Remaining salaried workers were required to take a 9 percent pay cut and "agreed" to have their salaries frozen for at least two years.

Over the next few years, under Beal's leadership, decisions were rolled out in the top-down style of command-and-control, all focusing on relatively quick fixes and short-term financial results. While the decisions were not always popular, most staff recognized the need for quick responses and tough measures. And there were positive moves as well. The Harley Owners Group (HOG) was created in 1983 as a means of communicating more effectively with customers and quickly grew into the world's largest motorcycle club. In 1984, Harley introduced the Evolution engine and the Softail product line, both of which quickly began making money for the company. Japanese-style manufacturing techniques—employee involvement, just-in-time materials delivery, and statistical process control—were introduced in the mid-'80s, and led to significant productivity improvements and decreased costs. By 1986 Harley's financial situation had rebounded, market share was increasing, dealerships were reengaged and their numbers growing, and the number of warranty claims was declining as a result of improvements in quality. The executive team decided to make an initial public offering. The offering was made in July and raised $25 million more than the underwriters had expected. The crisis had passed. By communicating the reasons to staff while quickly making the necessary tough decisions, Beals and his team had minimized resistance and maximized the financial benefits. Command-and-control had saved the day.

Clearly, the Commanding Dimension can be a powerful tool in a leader's toolkit.

Overuse of Commanding

Nonetheless, some words of caution regarding this Dimension are in order. For many executives and managers, Commanding is their dominant, if not exclusive, leadership tool. Appendix A describes two key factors that account for the prevalence of this leadership approach. What we want to emphasize here are the difficulties that attend an over-reliance on this Dimension.

We simply cannot afford the luxury of managing people in the same way as we have in the past.
—Stephen Croni, group personnel director, Rank Xerox

There may have been a time when this style worked—and worked well. But in today's business climate there are significant limitations on the settings in which this style is appropriate—a climate where information, not standardized work processes, is the lifeblood of the organization, where a more educated workforce expects more involvement in and satisfaction from their jobs, where global competition requires continuous innovation and change, where customer expectations for speed and quality of service have pushed the requirement for decision making down to the level closest to the customer, and where cultural shifts have made the commanding of "subordinates" offensive.

When leaders ignore these new realities and use a Commanding Dimension as their standard approach, certain negative consequences are predictable. Peter Senge describes a number of these when he states, "Top-down directives, even when they are implemented, reinforce an environment of fear, distrust, and internal competitiveness that reduces collaboration and cooperation."[3]

Additional staff problems caused by an inappropriate use of Commanding include emotional disengagement from customers, minimal compliance to job standards, elevated absenteeism, and high rates of turnover. Stated succinctly, the problem with relying solely on Commanding is this: you can command compliance; you can't command commitment.

The Harley story demonstrates that when employed well and in a proper context the Commanding Dimension *is* an important tool in the leadership toolkit. However, it is highly significant that Harley-Davidson's leadership team recognized the *limitations* of Commanding and consciously shifted away from it in the years following their financial crisis.

The prominence and overuse of Commanding by executives and managers creates problems in many companies, but that should not lead to an abandonment of its use altogether. What's needed is a solid understanding of its proper contexts and specific objectives so that the Commanding Dimension can be used when advantageous and abandoned when inappropriate. As Richard Teerlink says, "Unilateral decision making at the top, a clear chain of command and foot soldiers who take orders and execute someone else's plan meticulously—all of these serve well in the crisis mode but don't help the organization months or years after the fire is extinguished."[4]

When to Use Commanding

Table 1 describes the contexts and objectives appropriate for using the Commanding Dimension.

Table 1

AN OVERVIEW OF COMMANDING

Definition: Taking charge and seeking immediate compliance to quickly effect a desired result

Strategic Objectives

- To effect a quick result
- To give clear direction in an emergency or crisis situation
- To obtain immediate compliance
- To soothe people's insecurities

Appropriate Contexts

- When facing a genuine crisis or emergency
- To kick-start a turnaround
- When dealing with a problem employee with whom other approaches have failed

DIMENSION 2: VISIONING
Pointing the Way

Leaders manage the dream.

—*Warren Bennis & Joan Goldsmith,* Learning to Lead

We define Visioning as *creating and effectively communicating a clear and compelling picture of a worthwhile future for the group.* It is one of the most powerful and frequently used tools in the leader's toolkit.

Visioning at SAS

The story of Jan Carlzon's leadership at the helm of Scandinavian Airline Systems (SAS) in the 1980s is a notable illustration of the Visioning Dimension of leadership and its positive impact on staff morale, productivity, and company profitability. It also demonstrates that a Commanding approach is not the only way to deal with a turnaround situation.

In 1980, SAS was facing a loss of $20 million. SAS had, in fact, been in decline for years. A highly centralized, bureaucratic organizational structure that focused on detailed operating procedures, rationalization, and productivity practices was ill-equipped to deal with the profound changes affecting the industry. Ongoing deregulation of the airline industry was eroding SAS's monopoly over many of its destinations, and profit margins were rapidly shrinking. In the late 1970s, in an attempt to stop the financial bleeding, SAS senior managers introduced cost control measures that negatively impacted customer satisfaction (for example, they discontinued free meals, in-flight movies and music, complimentary newspapers, inexpensive drinks—all standard in the industry at the time). At the end of the 1970s, customer complaints were endemic; the SAS public image was tarnished, and staff morale and performance levels had plummeted.

This was the situation when Jan Carlzon became CEO. He faced a daunting challenge, to be sure, but by the end of his first year SAS showed a $54 million profit. SAS subsequently garnered two "Airline of the Year" designations, from *Fortune* magazine in 1983 and *Air Transport World* in 1984. Employee enthusiasm was once again high, customers were returning in droves, and profits continued to climb.

> *Few, if any, forces are as powerful in human affairs as shared vision.*
> —Peter Senge,
> The Dance of Change

Carlzon's skillful use of Visioning was a central factor in SAS's remarkable rebound. In Carlzon's own words, "The new energy at SAS was as a result of the 20,000 employees all striving towards a single goal every day."[5] What was that goal? Carlzon passionately espoused the centrality of customer service as the key to future profitability and framed SAS's new vision as the quest to become "the best airline in the world for the frequent business traveler."

Carlzon had already seen the power of shared vision in his tenure as the CEO of Sweden's domestic airline Linseflyg. There, Carlzon also led a successful turnaround, achieved through the wholehearted support of the company's management and staff. How had he gained this support? In Carlzon's estimation, "What made them work so wholeheartedly? I think it was because they all understood our goals and strategies. We communicated a vision of what the company could be, and they were willing to take the responsibility of making it work."[6]

At SAS, Carlzon employed a number of means to broadcast the new vision:

- Developing the catch phrase "moments of truth" as a way of reminding people of the importance of every customer encounter with the company and the vision of delighting the customer at each of those moments

- Quantifying these encounters in order to challenge SAS's staff with the magnitude of the task (Carlzon determined there were approximately fifty million "moments of truth" for SAS annually)

- Conducting high-profile, high-energy company events to promote the new vision

- Distributing to all twenty thousand employees a booklet titled "Let's Get in There and Fight," containing the vision and goals for the company

- Employing symbols to connect the vision to people's emotions

- Engaging employees in conversation as frequently as possible to share the vision (Carlzon estimates that in his first year, he spent half his time in the field talking to employees. He claims that "the word going around was that any time three employees gathered, Jan Carlzon would probably show up and begin talking with them.")[7]

Carlzon's effectiveness involved his use of several of the five Leadership Dimensions. But his deft use of the Visioning Dimension is what stands out in this remarkable turnaround, illustrating this Dimension's power in a crisis situation. As shown in Table 2, however, the use of this Dimension is not limited to crises. In fact, the Visioning Dimension is one that an effective leader will use frequently. The mundaneness of daily routine, the overload of information (some relevant, some not) most employees face, the very human tendency to lose focus, and the need to adjust to ever-changing circumstances all call for leaders to paint vivid, compelling pictures of the future and to connect people's current actions to the realization of that vision on a regular basis. Visioning is a critical Dimension of leadership effectiveness.

A successful vision tells a lucid story about what the company wants to be.
—Mark Lipton, "Envisioning Growth," Optimize magazine

Table 2

AN OVERVIEW OF VISIONING

Definition: Creating and effectively communicating a clear and compelling picture of a worthwhile future for the group

Strategic Objectives

- To move people towards shared goals/dreams
- To realize a new opportunity
- To unite a group around a significant challenge
- To increase or maintain employee motivation and enthusiasm

Appropriate Contexts

- When change requires a new vision
- When staff are losing or have lost their connection to the meaning and the value of the work
- When the group has lost its focus or sense of direction
- When responding to tragedy or crisis

When to Use Visioning

Table 2 provides an at-a-glance overview of the Visioning Dimension and the objectives and contexts that are appropriate for its use.

DIMENSION 3: ENROLLING
Getting Buy-In

People only support what they create.

—*Margaret J. Wheatley,*
Leadership and the New Science

Enrolling is *creating buy-in and commitment by genuinely seeking input or employing democratic decision-making processes, or both.*

Enrolling at Harley-Davidson After the Turnaround

Earlier in this chapter we explored the remarkable turnaround experienced at Harley-Davidson in the 1980s. That part of the Harley story provided a stellar example of the skillful use of the Commanding Dimension of leadership by the senior management team. The ongoing strength and growth of Harley-Davidson through the 1990s and into this century provide an equally valuable lesson in the power of the Enrolling Dimension.

What is notable about the Harley saga is the awareness of its leaders regarding the limitations of the Commanding style of leadership—the style used during the crisis phase from 1981 to1986. Richard Teerlink, CFO in the crisis years and promoted to CEO in 1989, was particularly sensitive to these limitations. He contended that a command-and-control leadership style could not be maintained if Harley-Davidson was to sustain its return to profitability and reach new heights. In an article written for *Harvard Business Review* in 2000, Teerlink recalled his early reflections in the days after the crisis: "I myself didn't have a plan for the company in my back pocket. I only knew that capturing the ideas of our people—all the people at Harley—was critical to our future success."[8]

Teerlink knew that to realize this level of participation, Harley management would have to treat its staff very differently than they had during the crisis phase. "They could no longer be privates, taking orders and operating within strict limits. We needed to push, and push hard, to create a much more inclusive and collegial work atmosphere."[9]

In the ensuing months, senior managers spent many hours discussing how they could achieve this goal. Teerlink credits the insights of an external consultant, Lee Ozley, who joined the company and became Teerlink's mentor, as providing the push and guidance toward actions that helped to create the participative atmosphere for which Harley is now renowned. Relying on Abraham Maslow's theories of motivation, Ozley convinced Teerlink and his team that in the absence of a crisis, people will typically resist programs or initiatives that are imposed on them but will readily commit to programs and initiatives they create.[10]

So, in late 1988 Harley's senior management team began a number of initiatives designed to elicit the ideas, concerns, complaints, and dreams of all its employees. These actions provide concrete examples of the effective use of the Enrolling Dimension and the genuine buy-in it can create.

The first step they took was to approach the union leadership in their Wisconsin plant, asking them to partner with management in creating a vision for Harley-Davidson. Seventy union and management leaders were asked for their individual ideas. Next, small groups were used to develop consensus around the best of these ideas. This process culminated in a three-day consultation with all seventy members present, which led to a written strategic direction for the company.

The implementation of the vision was not simple and required more significant shifts away from traditional management approaches. This being the first attempt at the use of Enrolling, the implementation and results were somewhat mixed.[11] But it did begin an important shift toward an Enrolling approach to leadership that eventually bore fruit at Harley.

Since this initial attempt at Enrolling, Harley's leaders have learned how to use it more effectively, and the results have been impressive. One particularly striking example was management's partnering with the two major unions representing Harley's employees in creating the Joint Partnership Committee for the development of its new facility in 1994. Overcoming historic union/management mistrust, this partnership jointly developed two goals:

- Continuing improvement in existing facilities
- Radically improving production in the new facility

Managers and union representatives learned to *work together* in making decisions and being accountable for them—even when the decisions were tough ones. While far from being a perfect partnership, it has nonetheless led to significant improvements throughout Harley and especially in their newest plant.

The ongoing strength and success of Harley-Davidson provides a powerful testimony to the positive outcomes that issue from a skillful use of the Enrolling Dimension.

Table 3

AN OVERVIEW OF ENROLLING

Definition: Creating buy-in and commitment by genuinely seeking input or employing democratic decision-making processes, or both

Strategic Objectives

- To gain commitment through participation
- To increase quality of products/processes
- To gain information needed for decisions

Appropriate Contexts

- When you need to get buy-in on a decision or direction
- When you need to improve quality
- When you need others' input to make a sound decision

When to Use Enrolling

To review the definition of Enrolling and when to use it, see Table 3.

DIMENSION 4: RELATING
Creating Harmony

It is impossible to estimate how many good ideas are abandoned every day as a result of difficult-to-manage relationships.

—*John P. Kotter,* Leading Change

Relating is *creating and sustaining harmonious relationships (1) between you and individual staff members, and (2) among staff members themselves.*

Relating on the USS *Benfold*

The goal of relating is the creation of harmonious working relationships characterized by *mutual trust, respect, and goodwill*—the three ingredients of a healthy, productive relational environment in the workplace. The use of the Relating Dimension has tremendous positive payoffs for both the leader and the organization.

Mike Abrashoff's leadership as commander of the USS *Benfold*, an awe-inspiring, guided-missile naval destroyer, provides an outstanding example of the skillful use and practical benefits of the Relating Dimension. Abrashoff's story has been profiled in articles in both *Harvard Business Review* and *Fast Company* and more extensively in his book, *It's Your Ship*.[12] Under his leadership, the *Benfold* went from having one of the worst retention rates in the navy to 100 percent reenlistment. With Abrashoff as its commander, the ship went from having one of the worst states of combat readiness to winning the coveted Spokane Trophy for best combat-readiness in the fleet, setting several new naval standards along the way and returning to the navy $600,000 of its $2.4 million maintenance budget!

> The most compelling sign of Abrashoff's success may be the smooth interaction that now exists among the ship's company. The Benfold's experienced department heads, its divisional officers (most of them fresh out of the naval academy or ROTC), and its enlisted sailors all show a deep appreciation of the ship's relaxed discipline, its creativity, and its pride in performance.[13]

What is particularly noteworthy is that Abrashoff's leadership was anything but command-and-control in its style and emphasis. In his own words,

> I had come to realize . . . that no commanding officer has a monopoly on a ship's skills and brainpower. There's an astonishing amount of creativity and know-how below decks, just waiting to be unleashed. To set it loose and make it flourish, an effective leader should neither command nor control; he should provide vision and values and then guide, coach, and even follow his people.[14]

As commander of the *Benfold*, Abrashoff employed several Leadership Dimensions, but none more masterfully than Relating. This reflects a very conscious decision Abrashoff made in his first few days as commander of the *Benfold*. Abrashoff had watched as the ship's crew cheered with pleasure as his predecessor left the ship, so bad had been the environment on board. He knew that the command-and-control style used by his predecessor and the standard navy leadership approach would not redeem the situation. Abrashoff vowed to "treat every encounter on the ship as the most important thing in the world at that moment."[15] This was the beginning of his conscious use of the Relating Dimension. Practical demonstrations of it followed.

For instance, Abrashoff took it upon himself to learn the name of *every single one* of the 310 crew members on board, meeting personally with each individual in his office. Many of his young crew members had never been in a commanding officer's quarters before. In addition to finding out their honest opinion of the good, the bad, and the ugly about conditions on the *Benfold*, Abrashoff inquired about their families, their reasons for joining the navy, and their career and educational aspirations. This simple, but time-consuming, practice began the development of strong bonds between crew members and their CO. Abrashoff continued this practice, having a get-to-know-you personal conversation within two days of the arrival of any new crew member. While still maintaining the discipline necessary on a combat ship, Abrashoff had also instilled a sense of the importance of each individual to him personally, regardless of their rank.

Abrashoff also worked to create a sense of community and harmony between crew members. The results of a survey of visible minorities and females on board demonstrate the positive impact of this new sense of community. The two groups were asked about their respective experiences of discrimination and sexual harassment. Only 3 percent from each group reported any negative incidents, a remarkably low incident rate compared to naval statistics in general. How does Abrashoff account for this? In his estimation, "That's not because I give long lectures on prejudice or sexual harassment—it's because I talk about the effects of community and about the need to cultivate unity and teamwork with as much care as we give to maintaining our equipment."[16]

One final example of the Relating Dimension from Abrashoff's *Benfold* experience is particularly powerful. Two months into his command, a hateful, racially motivated fight broke out on board between two black sailors and one white sailor. While it was within his rights to throw all three combatants out of the navy, Abrashoff chose a different tack. He was especially concerned not to lose the two black sailors, having previously learned that they had both joined the navy to get away from an environment of gangs, drugs, and violence. He conducted a disciplinary

hearing (during which he gained all three crew members' explicit acknow-
ledgment that they wanted to stay in the navy) and sentenced them to
forty-five days' restriction to the ship and forty-five days of extra duty.

But Abrashoff wanted to redeem these sailors, not just punish them,
to show them and everyone aboard that *anyone* can come back. So when
he and his master chief came across the two black sailors playing cards
together on a Friday evening during their restriction, Abrashoff challenged them to a game. A crowd gathered around, much good-natured
bantering took place, the two sailors felt redeemed, and the card game
became part of *Benfold* lore. One of the black sailors went on to become
a mentor to other young black sailors on the *Benfold*, the other went on
to college, and the young white sailor reenlisted at the end of his tour of
duty,[17] all of which speak to the power of the Relating Dimension.

When to Use Relating

Table 4 wraps up our discussion of the Relating Dimension's objectives.

Table 4
AN OVERVIEW OF RELATING

Definition: Creating and sustaining harmonious relationships (1) between
you and individual staff members, and (2) among staff members
themselves

Strategic Objectives

- To create harmony
- To create a sense of togetherness and community
- To increase the degree and quality of communication, trust, and
  openness in the group
- To enhance the informal information networks between groups

Appropriate Contexts

- When rifts in a team need healing
- When communication networks need to be improved or extended
- When problems in communication or teamwork are hampering the
  group's effectiveness or potential
- When stress is fraying relationships

DIMENSION 5: COACHING
Developing People

*The growth and development of people is the highest
calling of leadership.*

—Harvey S. Firestone, founder, Firestone Tires

Coaching is *developing an individual's potential and performance while aligning the individual's goals and values
with those of the organization.*

The cover story of the May 7, 2001, issue of
Fortune was titled "How to Manage Like Joe Torre."
The article profiled Torre's success as the manager of
the New York Yankees and offered six specific management principles Torre exemplifies that business managers would do well
to emulate. This article is part of a recent trend that draws parallels from
the world of athletic coaching to the business world. While the terminology of "the manager as coach" may be a recent phenomenon, the reality is
that many business leaders have been using a coaching style of leadership for decades. What was once an exceptional occurrence is now being
advocated as an essential aspect of effective business leadership. It has a
positive impact on organizational performance, individual staff motivation, leadership development, and retention of top staff.

Carole Cameron's story provides a glimpse of the power of Coaching. While working in the Human Resources Department of Nestlé
Canada, Carole had the good fortune to be managed by Phil Geldart, a
leader who utilized the Coaching Dimension with great skill. Here's her
story in her own words.

Coaching at Nestlé: Carole's Story
For ten years I had the pleasure and privilege of working closely
with Phil Geldart, who was at the time senior VP, Human
Resources, at Nestlé Canada. He had recruited me as a human
resources generalist, a position I was destined to soon leave
behind.

Phil had an innate ability to see the hidden, or embryonic, talents and skills of those around him and made a point of tapping into that potential. Fairly early on in my tenure at Nestlé, I was inspired by a talented facilitator in an in-house training program and thought that this could be an exciting next step in my own career. While I was still engaged in my regular duties, Phil found and created many opportunities for me to check out just what program design and group facilitation were like. He provided constructive feedback and asked those great, tough questions of me. Things like "What was the result you were after there? What else could you have done/said/asked at that moment?" He encouraged me to observe and learn from others who were also masters at what they did. "Watch Melissa in front of a group," "Go talk to Leslie about using that project management software," and "Listen to Susan when she's on the phone" were some of the concrete ways he helped me improve my knowledge as a would-be trainer.

When the opportunity to join the training team did appear, Phil told me, "You have the sensitivity and instincts to really feel what's going on in the classroom. This will make you a great facilitator." I hadn't really thought about these as skill sets, but you can bet I focused on tuning into them from then on.

Phil always provided specific, meaningful feedback. Instead of the generic "great job" type of encouragement, he would say things like, "That icebreaker was great. It was funny without being silly, not too long, and provided the energy in the room that we needed." Now, that kind of feedback I could use.

For my first major assignment as a training manager, Phil charged me with the responsibility of redesigning the three-day corporate orientation program. It needed to reflect recent strategic changes and new realities. This was a daunting task, to be sure, and I truly wondered why on earth he had assigned this task to me—new to the world of training and [with] very little design experience. This was a huge initiative and a high-profile program. I thought to myself, "Well, if he believes I can do this, then I guess I can." Lots of input, lots of feedback, a few stumbles, and lots of encouragement later, I did do it! And learned so much along the way. After this project, I certainly had a new appreciation for the phrase *stretch assignment.*

The lessons I learned from Phil helped me develop my skills as a trainer and deepened my confidence to move my career forward in the Performance Development Department. What I experienced in being coached was typical for all his staff. Phil always focused on developing his people.

Phil not only enhanced the lives and careers of his direct reports; he also used his coaching style to help create a corporate culture that was founded in respect for the individual and a commitment to the development and strengthening of others.

Phil introduced the entire national organization to the coaching principles he lived through a leadership program he developed called "Championship Management." Starting with the executive management team, then cascading through the organization to directors, managers, and supervisors, this twelve-module program encouraged the company's leaders to commit to "unleashing human potential" through formal and informal methods of strengthening others.

When Phil left Nestlé he left behind him a seamless succession in his own department, and an organization with a solid leadership base. This legacy is testament to the care, attention, and highly effective coaching displayed by this great leader.

Carole's account reveals many of the key aspects of the Coaching Dimension and its tremendous potential in an organization. These include increased loyalty, a wider leadership base, and retention of top-notch talent.

When to Use Coaching

Coaching is the appropriate Dimension to use in specific contexts and objectives, as shown in Table 5.

Table 5
AN OVERVIEW OF COACHING

Definition: Developing an individual's potential and performance while aligning the individual's goals and values with those of the organization

Strategic Objectives
- To connect a person's desires and talents to the group's goals
- To improve quality of production or service by a staff member
- To extend the group's leadership base

Appropriate Contexts
- When an employee wants to improve performance
- When the breadth and depth of the group's leadership need to be improved

CONCLUSION

Earlier in this chapter we defined effective leadership as *the process of achieving desired results through people's willing participation*, and we also introduced you to the five tools—the Leadership Dimensions—that leaders need in order to create and sustain that willingness. This overview of the five Dimensions has emphasized the *objectives* that govern the choice and use of each. We turn now to the related *tactics* a leader must employ to be effective in achieving those objectives.

CHAPTER 3

SOME ASSEMBLY REQUIRED

HOW TO BUILD A LEADERSHIP DIMENSION

'Twas the night before Christmas when all through the house
I searched for the tools to hand to my spouse.
Instructions were studied and we were inspired,
in hopes we could manage "Some Assembly Required."
The children were quiet (not asleep) in their beds,
while Dad and I faced the evening with dread.

—Anonymous

Remember Christmas Eve, desperately trying to assemble a child's toy? It didn't go well, did it? No wonder many of us think the three most dreaded words ever penned in the English language are *Some Assembly Required.*

Well, the 5-D Leadership model calls for some assembly, too, but don't worry. Leaders at all levels of all kinds of organizations have quickly developed effectiveness in all five Dimensions using the processes described in this book. It's much less like assembling that tricycle, and much more like building with LEGO® blocks. Building a Leadership Dimension is certainly not child's play, but it's not inordinately difficult.

LEGO® AND LEADERSHIP
Building Blocks of the Five Dimensions

Everyone who has ever played with LEGO blocks knows the secret of their success, if only intuitively. What makes LEGOS work is something the company calls "clutch power." When you snap two LEGO pieces together, they stay snapped. . . . It is clutch power that makes LEGOS such a flexible, adaptable toy.

—Charles Fishman, "Why Can't LEGO® Click," Fast Company

Several years ago LEGO blocks were named the toy of the twentieth century by a prominent association of British toy retailers, and by both *Fortune* and *Forbes* magazines. Most of us have fond memories of spending hours and hours as children building with LEGO blocks. In some of our executive teambuilding workshops we conduct an exercise where groups of five or six members have to construct out of LEGO blocks an object that represents how they want their organizations to be viewed in the community. It's always amusing to watch the businesslike demeanor of these very serious, high-level leaders being transformed into childlike joy and laughter as they allow themselves to "play" at work—and to watch them beam with pride as their group explains the representation they have constructed. Most of the time, the structures they create are quite clever, elegant, and meaningful.

The creation of a highly effective Leadership Dimension is similar to the building of these representational LEGO structures. In the same way that these constructions rise from the artful combination of simple blocks, a very powerful dimension of leadership results from the artful combination of relatively simple, straightforward actions.

Workshop participants don't always create stable structures with their LEGO blocks. Sometimes these teambuilding exercises are done under a very firm fifteen-minute deadline; participants rush to put the pieces together, but despite the "clutch power" of LEGO blocks, their hastily constructed edifices are unstable and come crashing down. Even though it's a child's toy, it does take thought and skill to assemble the pieces well.

5-D Leadership Structure

As you know, the 5-D Leadership components are *Dimensions*. At the foundation of each Dimension are *Building Blocks*, which are *actions*, the basic tools for effecting change. Actions have two facets: *intention* and *implementation*.

As with building with LEGO blocks against the clock, a thoughtless or mechanical attempt to use the Building Blocks will yield unstable results. While understanding the actions involved in each Building Block is relatively simple, it's in the application and combination of these actions that the real skill of leadership is shown.

The purpose of this chapter is to identify the discrete actions that together create a particular Leadership Dimension and describe indicators that show whether the *application* of these actions is being carried out skillfully. These indicators are called "signs of good or poor construction."

The remainder of the book will help you find ways to build on your current strengths to artfully apply the actions to accomplish your goals. As you read the descriptions of the individual Building Blocks of the five Leadership Dimensions, it is important to distinguish between the *intention* behind the action and the manner in which it is carried out—the *implementation*. While the intention is always the same, the implementation will be a unique application of your particular talents and strengths.

When building with LEGO blocks, you can choose the same size of block from many different colors and still end up with the same shape of object. Similarly, different ways of carrying out the same action can produce the same result. For instance, you can ask for people's ideas (one of the Enrolling Building Blocks) via email, meetings, or contests. The intent is to gather contributions; the implementation, the way you do it, is up to you and your team. This distinction will be important later, when we look at the process of leveraging your unique strengths to create a powerful Leadership Dimension in your unique setting.

DIMENSION 1: BUILDING BLOCKS FOR COMMANDING
Taking Charge Without Making Enemies

You don't lead by hitting people over the head. That's assault, not leadership.

—Dwight D. Eisenhower

As you learned earlier, the Commanding Dimension seeks immediate compliance to quickly achieve a desired result. As with all five Dimensions, *the goal is to use the Commanding Dimension in a way that maximizes the positives and minimizes potential negatives.*

There are two contexts in which the Commanding Dimension is typically the most effective response:

- Urgent situations, such as genuine crises or turnarounds, which typically demand a rapid response—the hallmark of the Commanding style

- Dealing with problem employees, *when other leadership approaches have failed*

In the first context, urgent situations, there often is no time for deliberation, relationship building, or consensus building. What is typically needed is a swift, definitive response.

In the second context, the problem employee, most cases of inappropriate or disruptive behavior can be remedied without resorting to a command to "comply or else!" A skillful use of the Relating Dimension often opens the door to being able to influence the staff member's behavior. But not always! There will be some situations where the only way to obtain an individual's productive behavior is to mandate and monitor to make sure it happens. And even here, there will always be a few individuals who fail to comply and must face the consequences.

These two contexts make up the domain of the Commanding Dimension. But even when you are facing a situation where Commanding is the best leadership response, the degree of skill in using this Dimension will determine the outcome. Let's take a look at the five Building Blocks that combine to create the Commanding Dimension.

Commanding Building Block 1: *Quickly determining priorities, based on available information*

Commanding requires a willingness to make decisions without the luxury of sufficient time to explore and research the situation thoroughly. When using this Building Block, you have to find a balance between speed and thoroughness, determined by how fast you have to act. The urgency of the need for action is the ultimate arbiter.

In a crisis, a positive outcome depends on your ability to assess and analyze the situation quickly and rationally and establish the right priorities for the actions to be taken. Does the situation call for immediate cost-cutting action or does it require an injection of finances into the marketing activities of the company? Should some of your employees be redeployed to critical functions or should they be laid off to save money? What is the correct sequence of activities for your group to carry out to deal with the pressing problems?

Commanding Building Block 2: *Making rapid, often unilateral decisions*

Commanding frequently requires the leader or a small cadre of leaders to make unilateral decisions that affect their entire team, department, or organization. The "need for speed" in responding to a crisis or a noncompliant staff member typically necessitates top-down decision making. In the case of a crisis, taking the time to get buy-in or to build consensus is not an option. In the case of a problem staff member, seeking agreement has already been tried without success. Furthermore, in either circumstance, it is the immediate organizational needs that are primary, not the emotional responses and personal preferences of the employees affected by the decisions. This requires a certain degree of confidence and willingness to "take the heat" for unpopular decisions.

Commanding Building Block 3: *Issuing clear directives with a brief business rationale*

In a crisis situation, once priorities have been determined and critical actions decided on, the next step is to issue *specific, concrete* directives that implement the decisions. In dealing with a difficult employee, your directive must make clear the behavior you expect and behaviors that are forbidden.

A brief business rationale for the directives is an essential component of this Building Block. In the case of an urgent situation, when the people you lead understand the necessity for and importance of the required actions, resistance and negative emotions are minimized and response time improves.

For example, recently in the Canadian division of a major multinational packaged-foods organization, the implementation team conducting the migration to SAP enterprise software was required to work extremely long hours for forty-two days straight. If the rationale for such extreme working conditions had not been made clear there would certainly have been a revolt. Fortunately, the team leader had explained the nonnegotiability of meeting the "go-live" deadline. While they may not have enjoyed it, the staff willingly rearranged their lives to meet the need because the rationale was clear.

In the case of a difficult employee, stating a brief business rationale for your corrective directives helps explain the impact of negative behavior and the absolute necessity of compliance. For instance, telling one of your direct reports that "outbursts of anger toward the team are unprofessional and unacceptable" is not likely to gain the agreement you need for this behavior to change. Your report may simply discount your idea of what is professional. It is likely to be far more effective to say, "Yelling at your staff in anger and using profanity with them is unacceptable. It's driving down their morale and increasing the number of mistakes they are making, and their bad feelings are getting passed on to our customers, who are complaining about the lack of customer service they are experiencing from your team. That's why these outbursts of anger are going to stop now. If you can't control your temper yourself, then you will have to get the help you need to do so." That directive, bolstered as it is by the business rationale, is more likely to be taken seriously. (This assumes that with a difficult staff member you are using Commanding as a last resort, not as your starting point. Ideally, you would have already used the Relating or Coaching Dimension, or both. In most cases, these approaches will achieve the desired result.)

Commanding Building Block 4: *Monitoring for speed of action and compliance*

Issuing directives doesn't guarantee compliance. Giving clear business rationales for these directives may increase the likelihood of compliance, but there is always a possibility of the directives being misunderstood or of delays in implementation. That's why Commanding includes a monitoring process to ensure that people are doing what is expected within the timelines determined.

Monitoring for compliance is especially important when there is resistance or negativity toward the directives. However, there is a clear distinction between monitoring and micromanaging. Monitoring measures outcomes and results. Micromanaging inspects the doing of the work.

Commanding Building Block 5: *Determining and enforcing consequences for failure to comply*

Noncompliance in a Commanding situation usually spells disaster. Whether it is a crisis situation or a staff member who is damaging morale and profits, there is no room for failure to comply. Thus, the willingness and ability to enforce predetermined consequences are necessary components of this Dimension, requiring courage and steadfastness. This is particularly true when dealing with a difficult staff member, where the consequences may include formal discipline or termination. Such situations may be emotionally unpleasant, involve union representatives, create hard feelings with other staff, or even lead to vindictive verbal attacks from the individual, but enforcing consequences is necessary.

All five of these Building Blocks are needed to use the Commanding Dimension well. See Table 6 for a visual representation of the five core Building Blocks of Commanding and indicators as to whether the Commanding Dimension is being used well or poorly.

Table 6
CORE BUILDING BLOCKS OF THE COMMANDING DIMENSION

1. Quickly determining priorities, based on available information

2. Making rapid, often unilateral decisions

3. Issuing clear directives with a brief business rationale

4. Monitoring for speed of action and compliance

5. Determining and enforcing consequences for failure to comply

Signs of Effective Commanding	Signs of Ineffective Commanding
▪ Immediate compliance with directives	▪ Resistance to directives
▪ Emotional relief among staff in a crisis situation	▪ Resentment and anger among staff in a crisis situation
▪ Priorities being followed	▪ Confusion about priorities
▪ Willingness to go the extra mile during the crisis phase	▪ Minimal compliance from staff, sabotaging behaviors

DIMENSION 2: BUILDING BLOCKS FOR VISIONING
Painting Pictures That Come to Life

Without vision, organizations have no chance of creating their future—they can only react to it.

—Jim Collins and Jerry Porras, "Organizational Vision and
Visionary Organizations," California Management Review

The Visioning Dimension seeks to create and communicate a clear and compelling picture of a desired future.

It is difficult to overestimate the importance of vision in a company. A clear and compelling vision provides focus, motivation, direction, and meaning. Because of its centrality to the success of an organization, the Visioning Dimension is one of the most frequently used tools in the leader's toolkit. The time invested in mastering the Building Blocks of this Dimension will reap huge rewards for leaders.

It needs to be emphasized that this Leadership Dimension is not reserved only for the upper echelon of leadership. Visioning is a Dimen-

sion that leaders *at all levels of the organization* need to use—and use frequently. As Collins and Porras state, "Vision setting should take place at
all levels of an organization and each group should set its own vision—
consistent, of course, with the overall vision of the corporation."[1] The
power and potential of Visioning in creating unity, enthusiasm, meaning, and commitment shouldn't be restricted only to top leadership.

Visioning Building Block 1: *Formulating with the group a compelling picture of a desirable future*

This Building Block comprises two key elements.

1. Painting a *compelling picture*

   As Peter Jensen, one of Canada's top corporate coaches, says,
   "Imagery is the language of performance. Our job is to help people
   see what's possible."[2] The more concrete and descriptive the picture
   is, the easier it is for people to believe in and commit to the vision.
   There is a world of inspirational difference between "We want to
   make great bicycle products" and

   The best riders in the world will be using our products in world-class
   competition. Winners of the Tour de France, the World Champi-
   onships, and the Olympic Gold Medal will win while wearing Giro hel-
   mets. We will receive unsolicited phone calls and letters from
   customers who say, "Thank you for being in business; one of your hel-
   mets saved my life." Our employees will feel that this is the best place
   they've ever worked. When you ask people to name the top company
   in the cycling business, the vast majority will say, "Giro."[3]

   Painting vivid pictures using images, analogies, metaphors, and
   examples is central to effective Visioning.

2. Envisioning a *desirable future*

   In this context, *desirable* means that the picture resonates strongly
   with the group members' values and aspirations. This is what gives
   Visioning its power. Making a significant contribution to the world,
   increasing knowledge, making peoples' lives better in some fashion—
   these are the kinds of aspirations to which people can commit and
   in which they will be willing to invest their best energy and effort.
   For a vision to inspire, unify, and sustain performance, it must con-

nect with individuals at this deeper level. The vision must be a concrete, vivid picture of a future that the group *wants* to create together.

Obviously, this means the leader must be in touch with those values and aspirations. In practical terms, this is best accomplished by involving group members in the development of the vision.

Visioning Building Block 2: *Continually and consistently communicating the vision*

In an information-overloaded work environment, leaders must continually communicate the vision to the group. It's generally safe to assume that you are undercommunicating the vision, not overwhelming people with it. Leaders need to use a variety of means and forums to repeat, restate, and reemphasize the vision.

Since a vision is typically communicated down through a number of levels, you must make sure that everyone is communicating that vision consistently. Mixed messages confuse people and dilute the unifying potential of Visioning. Leaders need to be sure that, together, they are communicating one message.

Consistency of the message is also demonstrated when the leader's actions are congruent with the stated vision. For example, let's say the vision emphasizes the blazing speed with which your company will now respond to both customer concerns and environmental challenges. To then take six months to approve financing on a proposal for new product research undermines that vision. Whether or not there are legitimate reasons for this delay, such a slow response will likely be perceived as discrediting the stated vision. As leaders, our actions need to be seen as an integral (and, perhaps, the primary) means of communicating the vision. If on occasion we must take actions that are seemingly inconsistent with the vision, the reasons need to be explicitly communicated.

> *Managers undercommunicate, and often not by a small amount. Or they inadvertently send inconsistent messages. In either case, the net result is the same: a stalled transformation.*
> —John P. Kotter,
> Leading Change

Visioning Building Block 3: *Freeing people to take individual and collective action to achieve the vision*

The intention behind Visioning is not to prescribe specific actions but to inspire initiative. The vision brings unity of focus and direction, not detailed directives. Certainly the leader(s) will want to develop a strategic plan for realizing the vision. However, the more freedom we give to the individual and/or group to take initiative and make decisions that implement the vision, the more commitment we will engender. It is in this sense that Warren Bennis and Joan Goldsmith say, "Leaders manage the dream."[4]

The essential task for the leader in this Building Block is to create the environment and remove the impediments for individuals and groups so that they can act. In *Leading Change*, John P. Kotter identifies four common impediments to effective employee initiative:[5]

- Organizational structures that are antithetical to the vision and get in the way of effective action (such as departmental silos or excessively bureaucratic approval processes)

- Lack of employee skills and training needed to perform the new tasks the vision requires

- Organizational systems not aligned with the vision that discourage employees from taking new action (for example, compensation structures and performance evaluation, promotion, or strategic planning processes)

- Managers and supervisors who act to undermine the vision and efforts by their staff to make it happen

Directly confronting all four of these barriers is a core function of this third Building Block of the Visioning Dimension.

Visioning Building Block 4: *Recognizing the contribution of individual and group activities in realizing the vision*

Most individuals need regular recognition from their leader to maintain peak levels of motivation.[6] This need is heightened when an employee is learning new skills and behaviors, or when actions involve the risk of failure or disapproval from others. In these circumstances, recognition of both the effort and any successes is important. Visionary leaders look for opportunities to reinforce actions and attitudes that move the group toward the realization of the vision. This is best accomplished through public recognition of both individuals and teams for their work in implementing the vision.

Implicit in this Building Block is the importance of refraining from criticizing and blaming individuals for their failures when trying out new ideas or behaviors. A supportive response that focuses on learning from the attempt for the future, rather than judging or criticizing the person for failing, is the most effective leadership response.

Table 7 summarizes the four core Building Blocks of Visioning, along with the signs of effective and ineffective use of this Dimension.

Table 7

CORE BUILDING BLOCKS OF THE VISIONING DIMENSION

1. Formulating with the group a compelling picture of a desirable future
2. Continually and consistently communicating the vision
3. Freeing people to take individual and collective action to achieve the vision
4. Recognizing the contribution of individual and group activities in realizing the vision

Signs of Effective Visioning	Signs of Ineffective Visioning
▪ Sense of hope and confidence about the future	▪ Lack of awareness of the vision
▪ Unified focus in the group	▪ Competing visions of the future
▪ Passion about the vision	▪ Confusion, indifference, or cynicism about the vision
▪ Alignment of the actions of sub-groups in achieving the vision	▪ Misaligned or contradictory actions by individuals and/or subgroups
▪ Group structures, processes, and leadership that support employees in realizing the vision	▪ Group structures, processes, and leadership that impede employees in realizing the vision
▪ Recognition of individual and group contributions in realizing the vision	▪ Lack of recognition of the relation between employee actions and realization of the vision

DIMENSION 3: BUILDING BLOCKS FOR ENROLLING
Leaving the Station with Everyone On Board

Most companies have huge repositories of undiscovered gold mines of ideas.

—*Hermann Simon, Simon, Kucher & Partners*
Strategy & Marketing Consultants

The Enrolling Dimension promotes participation in *idea generation* and *decision making*. Genuine commitment, better decisions, and ongoing improvements are three of the primary results a leader stands to gain with an adept use of the Enrolling Dimension.

Enrolling Building Block 1: *Eliciting and genuinely considering input, ideas, and suggestions from group members*

Numerous means exist for soliciting and recording the input from members of one's group. Email, town-hall meetings, informal or formal one-on-one conversations, regular staff meetings, focus groups, and even the now old-fashioned suggestion box are all mechanisms that can elicit ideas from your group members. Each has its advantages and disadvantages and it is usually wise to use a combination of methods. This allows you to account for the preferences of individual staff members—some may prefer face-to-face interaction, others a less personal process.

For any of these mechanisms to work effectively, those being asked for their ideas *must* perceive that their input is genuinely desired and will be taken seriously (so as not to lead to cynicism about the process). Your group members will unlikely be willing to give you their best input unless and until they believe you possess

- An attitude of humility regarding the limits of your own wisdom

- A belief that your staff members have valuable insights and ideas that can benefit the group

- A commitment not to "shoot the messenger" if they tell you things you don't like hearing

- A determination to understand the individual's point of view

Participative management without a belief in that potential and without convictions about the gifts people bring to organizations is a contradiction in terms.
—Max Dupree,
Leadership Is an Art

For Enrolling to work well, you must really have these attributes, not just feign the behavior. People will sense it if you are merely going through the motions. Genuineness is the foundation of trust, and people must trust you to enroll in your agenda.

It is difficult to keep up the act with something you don't really believe in. If you don't truly believe in the value of getting others' ideas, it will show up over time in your behavior—eventually you will stop asking for input.

Enrolling Building Block 2: *Implementing others' worthwhile ideas*

Ideas need action. One of the most powerful means of demonstrating our genuine belief in the value of others' ideas is to use them.

Of course, not every idea or suggestion a leader receives is going to be chosen. Not all ideas that surface will be good ones. Some may be clearly inappropriate or even dangerous (though we should not too quickly dismiss crazy ideas—there is a long history of breakthrough thinking that was initially perceived as crazy, stupid, or impractical[7]). Even when good ideas do emerge, we will want to select only the best of these. So how does a leader choose only the best ideas without discouraging future contributions from those whose suggestions are not utilized in a particular situation?

The solution is to have an idea evaluation process that is perceived to be transparent, fair, and effective. When people know that all ideas receive a fair hearing and are judged on their own merits, they can more readily accept that their idea was not the one selected.

As with the process of getting input, so too the mechanism used for evaluating ideas can take many forms (for example, a representational group can be formed to make the decision, or a virtual voting process using email or the company Intranet could be used). In deciding which particular evaluation vehicle to use, consider these factors:

- The time frame for making the decision

- The availability of the required technology for collecting and evaluating data

- Time available for the individuals to participate in the process

Even when proposing their own ideas, leaders can still seek the buy-in of their staff. For example, referring to a suggestion as "an idea" rather than "my idea" lessens the likelihood that people will concur with the idea because it comes from *the boss*, rather than on its merits. Asking if there are any holes in the proposed idea gives your staff permission to critique or develop the concept. Speaking of "the idea we came up with" rather than "the idea I proposed" encourages group ownership of the decision. These types of statements and behaviors elicit buy-in, even when the initial suggestion comes from you.

Enrolling Building Block 3: *Publicly crediting others when their ideas, innovations, or improvements are adopted*

Nothing destroys wholehearted participation and commitment faster than the boss taking credit for other people's ideas. Doing so virtually guarantees they will never again give you their best input and will be likely to harbor resentment and suffer low morale. Additionally, as other staff members learn of this behavior, they too are likely to resist any future attempts to gain their involvement.

Thankfully, most leaders have more integrity than to actually claim someone else's ideas as their own. But what is all too common is simply *failing to acknowledge the source* of the new idea or practice. It is difficult for most individuals to sustain enthusiasm and willingly take the time and energy to come up with suggestions for improvements unless it is acknowledged when they do so. A "what's the point?" atmosphere is soon created. There is much to lose when we fail to acknowledge others' contributions.

There is much to *gain* when we do praise others' contributions. When people know that they will be genuinely thanked and acknowledged (and, perhaps, receive some kind of reward, though this is not always needed), we deepen their commitment. We begin to create an atmosphere where people go above and beyond, giving their best energy to the group's success. This is the power of genuine recognition. There are so many vehicles for giving credit: newsletters, team meetings, company meetings, billboards, and memos. Keep these factors in mind when choosing your recognition tactics:

- The employee's preferences (not everyone likes to be singled out publicly!)

- The number of people affected by their idea

- The strategic importance of their contribution

The method of giving credit may vary; the importance of doing so does not.

Enrolling Building Block 4: *Facilitating consensus decision making*

Two aims govern consensus decision making: (1) achieving the best decision possible and (2) obtaining *genuine buy-in* from those involved. Both are important. Consensus is *not* a synonym for either watered-down or total unanimity. As we use it here, consensus simply means *overwhelming agreement.*

1. Consensus decision making is desirable when a leader lacks the necessary information to make the decision.

   In today's complex business world, often no one person has all the information needed to make the best decision. Frequently group members have the insights and ideas that the managers don't have access to. When Lou Gerstner Jr. took over as CEO of IBM, he was a virtual stranger to the information technology sector, having served previously at American Express and RJR Nabisco. Gerstner used the wisdom of his senior staff, who possessed a deep knowledge of the industry, and together they forged a consensus around the core challenges facing IBM in its critical days in the early 1990s. Gerstner knew his limits and made sure he had the expertise he needed around him. In an article for Harvard Business School's *Working Knowledge,* Gerstner states, "People at IBM were very smart. I didn't have to [look] outside."[8] He used consensus decision making to get agreement on the critical issues and then moved toward a new vision for IBM.

2. Consensus decision making is also useful when a leader wants to gain greater commitment to and buy-in of a goal.

Decisions reached together are more likely to be owned by all involved. Generally, when a decision is made for someone else, that person has less emotional commitment to it and may even resist it. If someone has been involved in the decision-making process and concurs with the decision, commitment to act on it wholeheartedly is usually very strong.

Facilitating consensus decision making depends on a wide range of activities and skills:

- Building trust and openness among group members

- Maintaining as much neutrality as possible

- Formulating with the group an initial proposal of the problem/opportunity/need

- Checking to make sure people are understanding each other's meaning

- Generating new alternatives through brainstorming

- Summarizing and restating the ideas on the table, areas of agreement, questions still to be resolved

- Guiding an evaluation of the merits of alternatives

- Checking to see that the selected idea/proposal is accepted by all

- Implementing a process for dealing with continued disagreement

The four core Building Blocks of Enrolling are shown in Table 8 with indicators of their effective and ineffective use:

Table 8

CORE BUILDING BLOCKS OF THE ENROLLING DIMENSION

1. Eliciting and genuinely considering input, ideas, and suggestions from group members

2. Implementing others' worthwhile ideas

3. Publicly crediting others when their ideas, innovations, or improvements are adopted

4. Facilitating consensus decision making

Signs of Effective Enrolling	Signs of Ineffective Enrolling
• High levels of participation and suggestions	• Low levels of participation and suggestions
• Strong sense of ownership of one's work	• Staff feel treated like children
• Free exchange of ideas (even unpopular ones)	• No sharing of ideas that challenge the status quo
• Satisfaction regarding the quality of decisions	• Frustration over lack of decision making or quality of decision
• Commitment to the mission/task	• Cynicism about the mission/task

DIMENSION 4: BUILDING BLOCKS FOR RELATING
Topping Off the Engine Oil

It's your job as leader to create an atmosphere that . . . transforms antagonism into creative energy.

—*John Kao*

The Relating Dimension seeks to create strong relationships (1) between the leader and a staff member, and (2) among staff members themselves. Its use fosters the interpersonal harmony necessary to sustain productivity.

Friction in your car engine is not a good thing. Without sufficient lubrication, metallic parts rubbing together will soon seize up and bring your vehicle to a grinding halt. The same can be said about organizational dynamics. Strong working relationships are the lubricant that keeps the work flowing smoothly and productively. Without them things often grind to a halt. This is true in terms of both relationships among group members and the relationship between a leader and the individual being led.

While some staff members can maintain high levels of productivity in an atmosphere of relational tension, unresolved conflict, or the absence of a sense of community, most employees cannot. When relationships among staff members are strong (characterized by mutual trust, respect, and goodwill), people are free to focus on the task at hand, information flows freely, and people have a motivating sense of collegiality. Most people need strong relationships in the workplace to maintain high levels of productivity.

Even more debilitating is the lack of a strong relationship between the leader and a staff member. In fact, research by the Gallup Organization has shown that the primary reason people leave organizations is a poor relationship with their manager/supervisor.[9] The quality of the relationship between an employee and his or her manager is the single biggest factor influencing motivation, commitment, and retention.

For these reasons, leaders frequently need to use the Relating Dimension. Let's take a look at the Building Blocks that combine to create this vital Dimension.

Relating Building Block 1: *Caring about the well-being of the whole person, not just what that individual contributes to the organization*

Workers have never enjoyed being treated in an impersonal fashion, as tools not humans, resources not people. What is different in our day is that many more employees are unwilling to put up with such treatment. Approaching staff members in such impersonal ways is sure to increase employee dissatisfaction, resulting in minimal effort on their part. But the opposite is also true.

Caring for the entire person is one of the ways we increase employee motivation and commitment. When our group members feel that they are valued as whole persons we gain their dedication and willingness to go the extra mile. Earlier, we mentioned recent research conducted by the Gallup Organization regarding the reasons people leave organizations.

This study ranked the top twelve factors in employee productivity and retention. Number five on their list is "My supervisor, or someone at work, seems to care about me as a person." In fact, ten of the twelve factors directly involve the quality of the staff members' relationship with their immediate managers.[10] Relating to people in ways that make them feel valued as a *whole person* is essential to long-term productivity (it also generally makes them much more amenable on those occasions when we do have to use the Commanding Dimension—people are more willing to be directed when they know their manager cares about their well-being).

How does a leader demonstrate a genuine concern for *the well-being of the whole person?* Stephen R. Covey, noted management consultant and author, is fond of saying, "In relationships, the little things are the big things." Demonstrating concern for the whole person is mostly a matter of little things:

- Using a person's name

- Asking how his or her weekend was

- Talking about his or her interests and hobbies

- Asking how work is going

- Talking about his or her family

- Discussing his or her career aspirations

There are occasions—for example, family emergencies or personal illness—when showing that we care for the whole person may involve more effort by the leader and, quite frankly, more inconvenience for the business. It is these occasions that test the genuineness of our commitment to care. However, the return in employee goodwill, respect, and loyalty is more than sufficient payoff. As with other aspects of leadership, the underlying attitude must be genuine. People can sense whether our actions are rooted in an authentic concern for them or in a "leadership technique" to get more out of them. Actions of concern without an attitude of caring foster cynicism and resistance. Technique without truth is barren.

Relating Building Block 2: *Providing encouragement and emotional support for the individual's or group's efforts*

This Building Block is about letting individuals and groups know that you appreciate their efforts (even when they fail) and their stresses during tough times. The business benefits to be reaped are immense: increased loyalty, effort, and commitment from your people.

In his article "Leadership That Gets Results," Daniel Goleman described the manner in which Joe Torre, general manager of the New York Yankees, attends to his players' emotions. One powerful example is the way he responded to Paul O'Neill, who chose to play in the deciding game of the 1999 World Series even though he had received news of his father's death that morning. Goleman writes, "At the celebration party after the team's final game, Torre specifically sought out right fielder Paul O'Neill. . . . [In front of the entire team] Torre made a point of acknowledging O'Neill's personal struggle, calling him a 'Warrior.'"[11] Torre knew that O'Neill had made a huge personal sacrifice for the sake of the team and made sure that he knew it was deeply appreciated.

Torre is a master of being aware of the emotional state of his players and providing encouragement and support, especially during tough times and slumps. He reaps the rewards of player loyalty and commitment.

For leaders in the workplace, this translates into words and actions that convey our confidence in our staff, our pride in their accomplishments, and our understanding for their failures. Of course, we must confront performance problems or inappropriate behavior. However, confrontations will have a much stronger chance of achieving the desired goal when they are conducted in a larger context of ongoing support and encouragement.

> *You must capture and keep the heart of the original and supremely able man before his brain can do its best.*
> —Andrew Carnegie

As mentioned earlier, it is important to draw a distinction between the *intention* of this Building Block and the *manner* in which the leader carries it out. Your personal style and strengths, as well as the preferences of the individual or team, will factor into the specific methods you use to demonstrate your encouragement and support. When Commander Mike Abrashoff sat down to play a game of cards with his two crewmen who were under discipline, his actions said, "I still value you."

In your case, providing encouragement and emotional support may mean

- Placing a heartfelt note of recognition and thanks on the person's desk or workstation

- Sitting down over coffee in the company cafeteria with a junior manager to talk about how he or she is coping with a problem staff member

- Making a telephone call to a geographically distant staff member who, you have heard, is feeling disconnected from the rest of the team

- Taking your team out for dinner at the end of a period of intense work and long hours

The options are many.

Relating Building Block 3: *Mediating conflicts to achieve mutually agreeable resolutions*

Mediation differs from arbitration—a response to conflict too many managers employ. In mediation, the parties themselves come up with the resolution but are guided through the process by the mediator. In arbitration the leader hears both sides and renders a decision by which both parties are expected to abide. Arbitration may seem like a fair and efficient process for conflict resolution, but there are two limitations that suggest it should be used as a last resort, not the initial approach. First, there is no guarantee that both parties will feel their interests have been satisfied. One or both may feel the decision rendered is unfair. Second, since the resolution is being imposed from outside, there is less commitment to following through on it. For these reasons, it is usually best to first attempt a mediated solution.

The primary indicator that mediation is needed is the inability or unwillingness of people to resolve an interpersonal conflict that is affecting their productivity. A leader needs to step in as a mediator in order to provide the perspectives and structures that will allow the parties to find a mutually satisfying solution that strengthens mutual respect and goodwill. These are the goals of the mediation Building Block.

Mediating a conflict involves a series of distinct steps:

1. Meet with the parties separately to gain an understanding of each point of view of the conflict and assess the level of willingness to collaborate through mediation to reach a mutually agreeable resolution.

2. Get the parties together and guide them to
   - Share their perspective on the conflict, clarify their underlying interests, and gain an understanding of the other's underlying interests
   - Generate a list of possible resolutions that satisfy all parties' underlying interests
   - Evaluate the possibilities based on criteria that everyone determines to be fair
   - Create a plan to implement the agreed-on resolution

3. Follow up to evaluate the success of the negotiated agreement

This process requires the leader as mediator to

- Maintain impartiality

- Help the parties *understand* each other (even if each *disagrees* with what the other is saying)

- Make sure the parties speak and act respectfully toward each other

- Push for specificity in clarifying underlying interests, generating concrete options, and creating detailed plans for implementation

Relating Building Block 4: *Conducting effective teambuilding*

Teambuilding requires much more than going white-water rafting together for a day.[12] It involves creating *ongoing* trust, openness, and camaraderie. The group leader must first model these characteristics. To promote the importance of these qualities while behaving in a critical, abrasive, guarded, or aloof manner is to sabotage the effort. The walk must match the talk.

Beyond *modeling* the relational characteristics desired in the group, the leader must also *promote* their development and actively reward their demonstration. Leaders will need to talk regularly about the kinds of team dynamics they want to see and why these are important. Generally, once these behaviors are characteristic of the group, they are psychologically rewarding in themselves.

Behaviors that seriously harm the group's relationships need to be confronted directly and quickly. Sometimes this means talking to the individuals displaying such behaviors and coaching them to use more productive behaviors. For instance, a team member who describes others' ideas as stupid or dumb needs to be shown how to offer criticism that focuses on the merits of the ideas without attacking another's intelligence.

Confronting negative behavior might involve reexamining and realigning the group's operational structures and reward systems to better reflect team values. For instance, a sales team leader might verbally promote the importance of cooperation in generating leads and the sharing of best practices yet actually reward only individual effort (such as offering a trip to Hawaii for the salesperson who has the best six-months sales record). The rewarding of individual rather than team behavior will likely result in the team members failing to be open, trusting, and cooperative. In this case, the driving force behind the unwanted individualistic behaviors is the misalignment of reward systems, not the immaturity or bad attitudes of team members.

Table 9 gives a visual presentation of the Relating Dimension and its four core Building Blocks, with signs that reveal whether the leader is using it well or poorly.

DIMENSION 5: BUILDING BLOCKS FOR COACHING
Upping Their Game

Growth exists in the plant, not the gardener. But good gardeners get a lot more growth out of the plant than bad ones do.

—Peter Jensen, Coaching for High Performance

Table 9

CORE BUILDING BLOCKS OF THE RELATING DIMENSION

1. Caring about the well-being of the whole person, not just what that individual can contribute to the organization

2. Providing encouragement and emotional support for the individual's or group's effort

3. Mediating conflicts to achieve mutually agreeable resolutions

4. Conducting effective teambuilding

Signs of Effective Relating	Signs of Ineffective Relating
• Warm, respectful relationships between leader and followers	• Distant or overly familiar relationship between leader and followers
• High degree of trust between manager/worker and between workers	• Failure to confront inappropriate behavior in the group
• Openness in communication	• Guardedness in conversation
• Lasting resolution of conflicts	• Conflicts "forbidden" or surfaced without resolution
• Individuals feel valued as a person, not just a worker	• Inappropriate behaviors not confronted and corrected

Coaching seeks to bring out the best in others in order to increase performance, productivity, motivation, and commitment. Coaching has been demonstrated to be a key means of retaining top talent and extending an organization's leadership base.

Many leaders fail to coach because of two misguided beliefs. The first is that it takes too much time. While it is true that coaching requires an initial investment of time with staff members, their consequent increased capacity to take on greater responsibility and produce higher-quality work soon offsets this investment. The second erroneous belief is that coaching is too complicated. You don't have to be a professional coach to use this Dimension effectively. As we shall see, the actions that build this Leadership Dimension are quite straightforward.

What, then, are the Building Blocks that form the Coaching Dimension?

Coaching Building Block 1: *Assessing strengths, weaknesses, motivations, and potential of individuals and the team*

A primary goal of coaching is to align the aspirations, interests, and abilities of an individual to the organization's needs, goals, and vision. This requires the leader to know well the talent and motivations of those being coached.

Practically speaking, this Building Block of Coaching requires a leader to find ways to become familiar with staff members' capabilities, interests, and aspirations. The two most basic tools for this are observation and discussion. Noting what tasks a person does well and with enthusiasm is the primary means of assessment. Sitting down to talk about what a person enjoys and dislikes about his or her individual and team responsibilities is the other basic. But please note, this type of candid discussion will work only if the individual senses that the purpose of this conversation is to get help, not to be penalized. Trust and goodwill must be present for such a coaching conversation to be worthwhile.

> *The command and control leadership style is rapidly becoming replaced with visionary coaches, coaches who empower their teams to turn their vision into reality.*
> —Dennis Grimm,
> PricewaterhouseCoopers

Formal assessments can also be helpful as an adjunct to personal observations and conversations. Here are just a few examples:

- Personality type assessments (*Myers-Briggs Type Indicator*® and FIRO-B® assessments)

- Emotional intelligence assessments *(EQ-i*®*)*

- 360° leadership effectiveness feedback tools *(The Leadership Circle Profile)*

When used in combination and with a qualified facilitator, these tools can add valuable insight and information for both the coach and the individual or team. Appendix 2 provides some cautions and suggestions about using these assessments with your group members and recommendations on finding qualified facilitators in your area to assist you.

Whatever means are used, the foundational Building Block of Coaching involves getting a clear picture of the strengths, motivations, and potential of the individual or team.

Coaching Building Block 2: *Providing appropriate "stretch" assignments for professional development*

This second block builds on the first. Stretch assignments are those that call for individuals to use their talents at a higher level than before. The leader must be able to judge how big the gap is between each individual's current level of expertise and what will be required in the assignment. The desired gap is one that will challenge the person without setting him or her up for failure. It is also important to make sure that the assignment requires *a higher use* of the person's talents, not *different* talents.

For instance, a staff member may be demonstrating strong logistical abilities in the planning and scheduling of projects. To assign the role of supervising a team project may actually require the use of interpersonal skills more than logistical skills. This may set the person up for failure if the interpersonal realm is an area of weakness. This is not a stretch assignment, but an ambush in the making!

It is occasionally appropriate to provide assignments that call for the use of skills and talents that a person has not yet identified. Most individuals have a greater repertoire of talents than they imagine. When placing a person in this kind of assignment, care must be taken to provide extra input and support (without micromanaging the individual). The goal is to discover new areas of talent. A full discussion of the skills and knowledge required to be successful, together with the resources and support available, is critical when previewing these types of assignments. A balance must be found between assuring people of your belief in their potential and giving them permission to try and perhaps fail.

Coaching Building Block 3: *Ensuring that effective performance feedback takes place*

Feedback means giving specific information to a person or team about what they are doing well and what they could do differently to improve. Often your role is simply to guide them to reflect on their performance and what they achieved. *The results of their efforts are what provide the feedback;* you are simply helping each person evaluate those results in a way that guides new learning and behavioral change. This is best accomplished by asking such coaching questions as

- How would you rate your overall performance? Why?

- What do you think you did well? What natural talents did you use?

- What did you not do well? Why do you think that is?

- How do you think you could improve your performance next time?

> *The greatest good you can do for another is not just to share your riches, but to reveal to him his own.*
> —Benjamin Disraeli, British statesman, prime minister

Good coaching pushes for specificity in the answers. Specific behaviors, skills, and results need to be identified for someone to learn and improve.

At times, the individual or team may not be able to pinpoint what specifically they are doing well and where they could make adjustments. In these cases, the leader must provide performance feedback that can help the person/team improve. For such feedback to be useful to the recipient it needs to be

- Nonjudgmental (avoids evaluating motives or character)

- Specific (focuses on specific actions, not generalities)

- Behavior based (describes what the person/team actually did and the impact of that behavior)

- Timely (as close in time to the actual performance as possible)

Coaching Building Block 4: *Using appropriate teaching and training methods for individual/team learning*

Leaders who coach make sure that individuals receive the training they need to do the work required. They also make sure that the methodology used fits the learning preferences of the person receiving the training. Some individuals learn best in the traditional classroom setting. Others would prefer to just jump in and try things out with someone giving them real-time feedback. Some individuals prefer to learn online by themselves; others prefer an interactive dialogue with their coach. When these preferences are accommodated, learning is faster, easier, and more complete.

How do you determine a person's learning preferences? Ask. Specifically, ask the person to describe two or three of his or her best learning experiences and see what commonalities emerge.

Coaching Building Block 5: *Discussing individual career aspirations and plans*

This Building Block focuses on a person's long-term performance development. These occasional conversations explore a person's career track and are designed to facilitate the individual's progression in skills and responsibilities. The key is to focus on the person's own aspirations. While it can be useful to suggest possibilities that a person may not have considered, it is the leader's responsibility to tap into the individual's vision and aspirations.

While focusing on a person's long-term career goals may seem irrelevant to the current demands of your business, there is, in fact, an immediate benefit to you. Demonstrating your concern for and commitment to an individual's long-term career satisfaction reaps you the immediate rewards of your employee's positive energy and personal loyalty, two factors that have a direct impact on current performance.

As you've just seen, the Coaching Dimension has five core Building Blocks. Again, a leader needs all five of these to use this Dimension well, as shown in Table 10.

CONCLUSION

This chapter has provided an overview of the Building Blocks of the five Leadership Dimensions. These Building Blocks are the actions that leaders use to achieve the objectives of each Dimension.

You may realize that you are already comfortable and proficient with most or all of the Building Blocks of one or more of the Dimensions. At the same time, you may realize that you have a serious deficit

Table 10

CORE BUILDING BLOCKS OF THE COACHING DIMENSION

1. Assessing strengths, weaknesses, motivations, and potential of individuals and the team

2. Providing appropriate "stretch" assignments for professional development

3. Ensuring that effective performance feedback is provided

4. Using appropriate teaching and training methods for individual/team learning

5. Discussing individual career aspirations and plans

Signs of Effective Coaching	Signs of Ineffective Coaching
▪ Individual/team feels appropriately challenged	▪ Individual/team is set up to fail through inappropriate assignments
▪ Individual/team feels supported but not micromanaged	▪ Individual/team feels either micromanaged or abandoned
▪ Individual/team learns effectively, increasing performance levels	▪ Individual/team learning is minimal or nonexistent
▪ Individual/team understands and values the importance of their contribution to the work	▪ Feedback demotivates or frustrates individual/team
▪ Leadership base of the group continues to expand	▪ Leadership vacuum or need to import external leaders exists

of Building Blocks for several of these Dimensions. If an effective leader is able to shift between these Dimensions as required by the context, what are you to do when you lack the needed Building Blocks? To put it another way, "What do you do when you're a few blocks short of a Dimension?" The next chapter provides the answer.

CHAPTER 4

WHEN YOU'RE A FEW BLOCKS SHORT

THE ARCHIMEDES PRINCIPLE

*Each player must accept the cards life deals him or her.
But once they are in hand, he or she alone must decide
how to play the cards in order to win the game.*

—*Voltaire, historian and writer*

Certain Building Blocks may have resonated strongly with you as you were reading Chapter 3. You could see yourself naturally doing what was described, or perhaps you remembered past occasions when you used that Building Block effectively. Maybe some of these Building Blocks seemed like quite a stretch for you. So, as you contemplate using a particular Leadership Dimension, you may be thinking, "I'm short several of the Building Blocks for this Dimension. What do I do now?"

You don't need to live a life of regret, wishing you were someone else who was naturally talented at that Dimension. Nor do you need to devote hours and hours of concentrated effort trying to develop abilities that simply are not your strengths. *It is entirely possible for you to be a truly effective leader and use all five Leadership Dimensions well, with the strengths you already have.*

This assertion runs counter to some conventional leadership development practices, an approach we call "working harder, not smarter."

Because that approach is still found in some practices of leadership development, it's worth examining it in some depth to appreciate the simplicity and power of the 5-D Leadership approach.

WORKING HARDER, NOT SMARTER
The Weakness of Traditional Leadership Development

The point here is not that you should always forgo . . . weakness fixing. The point is that you should see it for what it is: damage control, not development.

—Marcus Buckingham & Donald O. Clifton,
Now, Discover Your Strengths

The way conventional leadership development is customarily practiced has two serious liabilities: The first is an overreliance on classroom-style learning. The second is an emphasis on trying to develop weaknesses into strengths. Let's consider each of these.

Classroom-Style Learning

A great many leadership development programs require extensive time spent in the classroom learning about leadership. While a thorough understanding of conceptual frameworks (for example, organizational systems, change management processes, the dynamics of high performing teams, current business and political trends) is important for leadership effectiveness, it is not sufficient. *Knowing* and *doing* are two very different things. Knowing the rules of chess and reading some of the strategies used by Bobby Fischer or Garry Kasparov won't turn someone into a chess master. The only way to become a good chess player is to play the game. Similarly, it is the adept application of leadership concepts and skills that creates leadership effectiveness, not merely awareness.

Regrettably, those outmoded leadership development programs spend very little time actually applying the concepts and refining the practical skills of leadership during their classroom time. Even when there is the opportunity to try out new skills during the program, integrating them back into the leader's actual work setting is left largely to the individual's determination and good fortune. To be sure, many leadership development programs are now offering postprogram coaching as an *option*. This is certainly a step in the right direction, but it isn't enough. Performance coaching should be an *integral component* of leadership development, not an *optional feature*.

Several recent studies have demonstrated and quantified the value of "coaching integrated with classroom" over the more traditional classroom-only method. One such study, published in the prestigious *Public Personnel Management Journal*, reported the results of a leadership development program conducted with thirty-one executive managers. Classroom instruction alone accounted for a 22.4 percent increase in managers' productivity. However, when the same program was followed by eight weeks of executive coaching, productivity gains skyrocketed to 88 percent.[1] Several other studies have documented the tremendous value of integrating coaching with more traditional classroom-heavy approaches.

Focus on Conquering Weaknesses

The second—and more serious—problem with antiquated leadership development practices is the emphasis placed on overcoming one's weaknesses.[2] Typically, leadership development programs begin with a process of rigorous self-assessment. Minimal attention is given to identifying strengths; the process typically emphasizes the discovery of a leader's current weaknesses and culminates with the creation of a thorough, detailed plan for turning those weaknesses into strengths (a plan that is often left to the individual to implement and evaluate alone).

> *But there are advantages to being elected president. The day after I was elected, I had my high school grades classified Top Secret.*
> —Ronald Reagan, speech, June 19, 1986

We believe this philosophy of working hard to overcome weaknesses is both misguided and ultimately counterproductive. It is a case of working harder, not smarter. Though it *is possible* to improve performance in an area of weakness, the improvement is typically insubstantial. *Focusing time and energy on creating a strength out of an area of weakness denies our human nature.* Skills that do not use your natural abilities take much more effort to develop and rarely rise above the level of mediocrity, a reality rooted in the way your brain works.

The brain functions by means of interactions between networks of synaptic connections.[3] By the time a person reaches age three, there are literally billions of these connections in his or her brain. During childhood, partly as the result of our genetic makeup and partly as a result of life experience, certain patterns of synaptic connections get used more frequently than others. As with muscles, these neural networks become stronger with use. Connections that are used less frequently are eventually pruned away, freeing up precious biochemical resources in our brains for the connections that remain. Your brain actually creates its own preferences and strengths. These neural connections determine much about us, including our personality traits, learning preferences, interests, and natural abilities.

By the time we reach adulthood, our neural patterns are virtually set. Learning that draws on these existing connections is easy and rapid. Learning that requires the development of new neural connections is much more arduous, requiring substantial energy, effort, and repetition. And the results are typically meager.[4] Marcus Buckingham and Donald Clifton point out the futility of this approach: "Without underlying talent, training won't create a strength. Also, repetition in an attempt to carve out new connections is simply an inefficient way to learn. . . . Your body has to expend relatively large amounts of energy creating the biological infrastructure . . . to create these new connections."[5]

It makes little sense to try to develop areas of weakness as the primary road to greater leadership effectiveness. It's like trying to move a boulder using a six-inch lever. You're working against natural principles and wasting precious time and energy resources. The results are likely to be minimal at best.

These two aspects of traditional leadership development—a classroom-heavy learning methodology and a focus on overcoming weaknesses—render it an ineffective approach. This leads us to the *Archimedes Principle for Leaders*, a fundamentally different way to develop leadership effectiveness. Why do we refer to it as the Archimedes Principle? The answer to that requires a brief lesson in the history of science, or more specifically, the principle of leverage.

THE ARCHIMEDES PRINCIPLE
Using Leverage to Move the World

Give me a place to stand, and a lever long enough, and I shall move the world.
—*Attributed to Archimedes, 230 BC*

Archimedes (287–212 BC) is generally ranked as one of the three greatest mathematicians of all time, along with Sir Isaac Newton and Carl Friedrich Gauss. In his own day he was referred to as "the wise one," "the master," and "the great geometer." He was a superb engineer (credited with numerous inventions, including the Archimedes screw, a miniature planetarium, the compound pulley, and several machines of war) and his contributions to mathematics include the discovery of the laws and principles of mechanics, buoyancy, hydrostatics, specific gravity, and the lever.

Levers had been in use long before the time of Archimedes. The first levers were probably logs or branches used by our ancient ancestors to lift heavy objects. Archimedes' contribution lay in determining the principles that govern their use. Consequently, he was able to maximize their effectiveness.

Legend has it that on one occasion he made the claim to Hiero II, king of Syracuse, that if he had a lever long enough and could go to another planet, he could move the earth itself. Hiero, a close friend, was astonished by this claim and asked Archimedes to prove his assertion. As the story goes, in the harbor at Syracuse lay a ship that had proved impossible to launch, even through the combined efforts of all the men of the city. Archimedes built a machine that used a combination of levers and pulleys that allowed him to move the ship single-handedly from a great distance away.

That is the power of leverage. Leverage lets us move things that would otherwise be physically impossible to move. Leverage allowed the great pyramids of Egypt to be built, a feat of engineering that still astounds. Leverage is a key principle taught in jujitsu that allows a smaller opponent to defeat someone much bigger and stronger.

Archimedes' statement "Give me a lever long enough, and a place to stand, and I shall move the earth" dramatically highlights the power of

Figure 1
THE ELEMENTS OF LEVERAGE

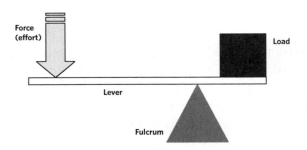

the simple lever. It's a power we use daily without even thinking about it. Using a crowbar to rip out that tree stump in your backyard is an example of leverage. Bicycle brakes work because of leverage. Hammer claws, scissors, pliers, and bottle openers all use the effort-multiplying power of leverage. Figure 1 illustrates the elements of leverage in its simplest form.

THE ARCHIMEDES PRINCIPLE FOR LEADERS
Leveraging Your Strengths to Move Your World

Here is a philosophy of boldness to take advantage of every tiny opening toward victory.

—Arnold Palmer, U.S. championship golfer

Leverage multiplies the effects of your effort, allowing you to achieve significant results with minimal effort. It is this principle that defines 5-D Leadership development. We think of it as a leadership application of the Archimedes Principle. Restated, the Archimedes Principle becomes:

Choose the appropriate Leadership Dimension and apply your natural strengths, and you can move your world.

This principle answers the question that is the focus of this chapter: what do you do when you seem to be short of the natural abilities that would be associated with a particular Building Block?

The answer is to *leverage the strengths you already possess.* This is the secret of the Archimedes Principle for Leaders that allows you to truly move your world.

It is important to emphasize how different this is from traditional leadership development. The quickest and most effective way to become a better leader is to find ways to apply your natural abilities when utilizing the Leadership Dimension that a situation requires. This approach—leveraging your natural strengths—allows you to work with the way your brain works, making your development fast, effective, and satisfying.

In an article titled, "Natural Talents: An Argument for the Extremes," David Feldman and Tamar Katzir reference a statement made by Irving Rosen, principal violinist of the Philadelphia Orchestra's second violin section. Commenting on a recent performance by the then eleven-year-old Midori, Rosen stated, "If I practiced three thousand years, I couldn't play like that. None of us could."[6] Rosen's comment recognizes what most of us accept as evident. Talent is inborn, and its development is what separates truly great performance from the merely competent. In the first part of this chapter we discussed the problem with trying to overcome weaknesses: it runs counter to the way your brain actually works. The flip side of this is also true and is the key to our methodology of leadership development. As Francoys Gagné points out, "Aptitudes or gifts . . . show themselves . . . through the facility and speed with which individuals acquire new skills in any given field of human activity. The easier or faster the learning process, the greater the natural abilities."[7] When you draw on your natural abilities, learning new skills is faster and easier and the level of excellence you can reach is much higher.

The distinction between ability and skill is an important one in 5-D Leadership development. *Skill* refers to a highly effective pattern of behavior developed over time. Thus *skill* is not synonymous with *ability*. In fact, it is possible to develop a certain degree of skill without having a natural ability for a given action. For example, individuals who do not have a natural ability for logistical organization can usually develop a functional level of skill in creating and maintaining a filing system that allows them to preserve and retrieve information when needed. Through determination, practice, and time, most people can achieve competence in numerous areas. But competence is not excellence. And the time and energy required to achieve competence is typically excessive when compared to the level of skill achieved.

> **There has never been a great performer who was not also blessed with great natural ability.**
> —David Feldman & Tamar Katzir, "Natural Taents: An Argument for Extremes"

The dynamics of learning are completely different when the learning draws on our natural strengths. The learning is easier, the results are superior, and the process is enjoyable. *Why is this so?* Well, that takes us back to our earlier discussion of the way the brain works. Neurological studies during the past ten years have revolutionized our understanding of cognitive processes. One of the key findings is that the brain has developed many powerful connections that create our natural abilities. Thus, if learning a new skill utilizes these neural pathways, the process is far easier and much more enjoyable. In cases of child prodigies, the almost obsessive desire to do the activity is one of the clearest early markers of a profound level of talent.[8] The neural networks in these children are so strong that they are compelled, as it were, to pursue activities that allow them to utilize these connections. While most of us will not rise to the level of genius, the pleasure we experience when using our natural strengths is still pronounced. We are "wired" for excellence *and enjoyment* when we use our strongest neural connections, our signature strengths.

This is the neurological basis for applying your natural strengths to leverage your leadership effectiveness. This methodology works *with* human nature, not against it. We recognize, however, that the *application* of this approach may not be so apparent, so to make it more concrete, let's look at a hypothetical example of leadership development using the Archimedes Principle for Leaders.

Archimedes and Leadership Development: Bill's Story

Bill is the head of a large division in a company facing a major reorganization. He has been mandated to decide who in his division should be retained, who should be laid off, and who should be reassigned in order to meet specific cost-cutting financial targets. He has six weeks to reach a final decision. As he considers this difficult situation, Bill decides he needs to use the Enrolling Dimension with his senior managers—both because he *needs* the insights his managers can provide and because he *wants* them to strongly support the decisions they will be implementing.

Given his personality, Bill's *natural preference* when enrolling his managers would be to ask them to send him the relevant data and their recommendations via email and then make the final decision himself. In this case, however, facing decisions that are financially and strategically critical, he decides that it would be better to gather all of his managers together face-to-face for a series of meetings. Furthermore, knowing that the final decisions will require his managers to lay off or lose some good people, he anticipates this will likely be an emotionally intense and painful series of discussions.

Bill then turns his attention to the specific Enrolling Dimension Building Blocks he will need. In these circumstances, he decides the critical Building Block is *facilitating consensus decision making.* He recognizes that he has three serious weaknesses that would seem to make this Building Block unnatural for him:

- He is not good at maintaining emotional neutrality in intense discussions
- He gets impatient with group process
- He is uncomfortable with conflict

Given these personal weaknesses and the futility of trying to turn them into strengths, how might he leverage his strengths to accomplish this goal? Let's say that four of Bill's greatest strengths are

- Storytelling ability
- Genuine concern for people
- Willingness to let others lead
- Ability to synthesize information

How might he leverage these to use this Enrolling Building Block effectively?

Both his *storytelling ability* and *genuine concern for people* could be used to connect emotionally with his staff at the very beginning of this decision-making process. Storytelling is one of the most powerful ways to enroll people emotionally. And when people sense you genuinely care about them, they are much more likely to cooperate with you and commit to the work. So Bill could begin by recounting a time in his managerial career when he had to make the painful choice of laying off good people whose families depended on their employment. He could then convey his awareness of how difficult these decisions may be for his team.

The next thing Bill could do is draw on his strength of *being willing to let others lead.* If there is someone on his team who has a natural strength for facilitating group decision making, Bill could ask (well in advance) that person to take the lead in actually facilitating the process. This is not abdicating responsibility. Bill is still the final authority on the team and can exercise that authority if it is necessary. However, being the official leader does not mean he has to be the one who actually does the facilitating. He just needs to make sure it happens.

Should there not be anyone on his team with strong skills for facilitating group consensus, Bill could choose to lead the discussion himself and still draw upon his willingness to let others lead. For instance, at the beginning of the process, he could openly acknowledge that at times he may lose his impartiality, grow impatient with the process, or want to suppress or ignore conflict. He could *ask others to speak up and let him know when this is happening to the detriment of the process.* It would be important for Bill to thank individuals when they actually do this, reinforcing that he genuinely does want this feedback.

Finally, drawing upon *his natural strengths for synthesis,* Bill could provide a valuable service to the process by occasionally summarizing the information and ideas of the group. If the process takes several meetings (as is likely), Bill could employ this strength in between sessions by informing his team of key trends, themes, concerns, or problems that have since crystallized in his thinking and that will need to be discussed at the next meeting.

This example of the Archimedes Principle for Leaders is a hypothetical one, so you may still be wondering, "Does leveraging your strengths really work? Can someone really leap forward quickly in their leadership effectiveness by using this methodology?"

The answer is "Absolutely." Daniel's story provides a real-life case that demonstrates the Archimedes Principle at work.

The Archimedes Principle at Work: Daniel's Story

Daniel had been working as a divisional director for a distribution company for three and a half years when, on the recommendation of his VP, I [Ellen] was brought in to coach him. Daniel's VP was deeply concerned about the negative impact that Daniel's brusque, no-nonsense, "just-get-to-the-point" interaction style was having in the company. The VP framed it this way: "He's really great at what he does. I just can't get anyone to work with him!" By the time I started coaching him, Daniel had succeeded in alienating virtually everyone with whom he needed to work.

In his position, Daniel had no direct reports. Rather, he was involved across many departments, sometimes as a project consultant, other times leading the project team itself. Because of his abrasive relational style, Daniel's peers and other staff with whom he interacted often felt treated as cogs in the machine, interruptions in his busy agenda, or miscreant children—and sometimes all three!

Those who absolutely *had* to work with him tended to resist his directives and requests, and minimized contact with him whenever possible, creating significant information gaps and delays. Frequently, Daniel ended up having to chase people for reports they were supposed to have turned in to him.

The upshot of this was significant. Several projects stalled and others had to be redesigned, wasting time and money and irritating customers. Daniel's VP realized that something had to change.

When we met for the first coaching session, Daniel eventually admitted that his relational style was a problem. He was assuming we would spend hours working on his becoming more empathic, being more patient with people, being warmer and more "chit-chatty." Daniel knew he lacked these characteristics but clearly did not seem motivated to develop them. However, once I was able to get Daniel to see that by learning to use his *existing strengths* to connect with people first and *then* get down to business, he could actually achieve more in less time, he became sincerely committed to the process. The focus then shifted to finding strengths he could leverage to build better relationships.

A First Natural Strength

As I interacted further with Daniel, I observed that in addition to his direct, task-oriented conversational style, he had a good sense of humor. His analysis of the problems he was facing was laced with wit and occasional humorous, self-deprecating comments. When I pointed this out to him, he was surprised that I thought this was significant. He had never thought to use this natural strength to create more effectiveness in both the Relating and Enrolling Dimensions of Leadership, Dimensions that were sorely needed in these circumstances. For Daniel, humor was an indulgence, not a leadership strength.

We discussed how he might use his humor to help break the ice before getting down to business and assigning work when meeting one-on-one with others. We talked about how he could interject his self-deprecating humor into team meetings, letting others see him more as a real person, rather than a business machine. We talked about how he could, during meetings, instead of blurting out his frustration with the slow pace of the meeting, make a humorous comment about the situation that got people chuckling but also made the point (we also discussed the difference between sarcasm and light humor!). It's important to note that I didn't try to turn Daniel into a relationship-oriented person. This he would never be. But neither did he need to be. Simply by introducing his natural humor, especially self-deprecating comments, he got people to begin to relax around him.

A Second Natural Strength
Daniel was able to leverage a second area of strength to improve his relationships with others: his time-management skills (not an obvious strength to leverage into relationships). When people came to talk to him, rather than getting frustrated if they seemed to be meandering or giving too much extraneous detail, Daniel would now frame the discussion up front by saying something like, "I only have five minutes until I have to get to a meeting. Can we discuss your concern in that amount of time, or should we schedule some time later?" This alerted people to be focused, and since most people did not want to postpone their meeting, they were more concise, which lowered Daniel's frustration level.

Additionally, rather than just being irritated by others' seeming inefficiency, Daniel started making suggestions (softened through the use of his humor) about how others could make better use of their time. Rather than lecture, he gave examples of what he did to manage time efficiently—often a humorous story of how he had learned what to do the hard way in the past. Consequently, others began to improve their own skills, especially when leading team meetings.

Over the course of a few weeks, his working relationships improved significantly. People stopped avoiding him and started cooperating more willingly. Reports began to be handed in on time, the reciprocal flow of information and ideas increased, and projects were being completed on schedule. Team meetings flowed more smoothly and Daniel even started to enjoy some of the banter and momentary diversions from the agenda. Soon after our coaching sessions ended, one of his relationally talented but rather disorganized colleagues asked him to partner with him on several key projects so they could play off each other's strengths. This was a far cry from the previous days when people sought to avoid him.

Daniel's success in leveraging his strengths had significant payoffs for both him and his organization. Only two months into our coaching process, his VP informed me that during a project debriefing session, five out of six directors specifically acknowledged his positive key role in the success of their projects. And months later, Daniel reported, not only were projects getting done on time and with excellence, but he was enjoying his work more than he had in many years!

Daniel did not have to become a relationship-oriented person to use the Relating Dimension effectively. What he *did* need to do was learn how to leverage his strengths while using the appropriate Leadership Dimension.

Does leveraging your strengths instead of trying to overcome weaknesses really work? *Ask Daniel.*

Will it work for you? *Absolutely.*

CONCLUSION

You will need a few things in place before you can start to use the Archimedes Principle for Leaders. First, you have to have a thorough understanding of your natural strengths and understand which of the five Dimensions are your natural Dimensions. This is the focus of the next section of the book. The second thing you will need is to be able to read your context clearly and know which of the Dimensions are most appropriate in the various leadership situations you are facing. That capacity will be the focus of the book's third section. The final section will bring it all together, exploring specific ways you can leverage your strengths in your unique leadership setting.

2

KNOWING YOURSELF INSIDE OUT

In the previous section, we demonstrated that the key to lasting leadership effectiveness is the ability to *shift* among Leadership Dimensions in order to match the demands of the immediate context. Using examples, we explored the particular contribution of each of the five Leadership Dimensions, detailing the specific Building Blocks of each.

Now, let's go through the steps of determining your primary leadership strengths (**Chapter 5**) and natural Leadership Dimensions (**Chapter 6**).

DISCOVER YOUR LEADERSHIP STRENGTHS

TOOLS FOR SELF-AWARENESS

Knowing others is intelligence;
Knowing yourself is true wisdom.
Mastering others is strength;
Mastering yourself is true power.

—Lao Tzu

Lao Tzu may have lived thousands of years ago, but his sage advice is just as relevant today. Knowing yourself *is* true wisdom. This chapter will take you through a five-step process to increase your self-knowledge concerning your leadership strengths. This process, detailed in Figure 2, will give you a solid foundation for developing true power as a leader—self-mastery based on self-awareness.

Figure 2

THE PROCESS FOR BECOMING AWARE OF YOUR LEADERSHIP STRENGTHS

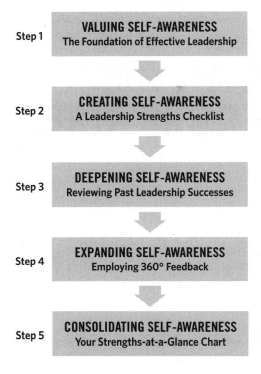

Step 1 — **VALUING SELF-AWARENESS**
The Foundation of Effective Leadership

Step 2 — **CREATING SELF-AWARENESS**
A Leadership Strengths Checklist

Step 3 — **DEEPENING SELF-AWARENESS**
Reviewing Past Leadership Successes

Step 4 — **EXPANDING SELF-AWARENESS**
Employing 360° Feedback

Step 5 — **CONSOLIDATING SELF-AWARENESS**
Your Strengths-at-a-Glance Chart

VALUING SELF-AWARENESS
The Foundation of Effective Leadership

Like the physician, it is important for the leader to follow the maxim "know thyself" so that he can control some of the pernicious effects he may create unwittingly. Unless the leader understands his actions . . . he may be a carrier rather than a solver of problems.

—*Warren Bennis & Philip Slater,* The Temporary Society

Self-awareness is the foundation of effective leadership. This statement is true on many levels. When leaders are highly self-aware, they are able to choose environments that fit their values, priorities, and talents—enhancing their effectiveness and helping to avoid burnout. The more self-aware you are, the less you tend to react blindly to circumstances and people that "push your buttons." Self-awareness keeps you from being blind to the harmful impact of your actions (see Monique's story, next).

Self-Unawareness and Poor Morale: Monique's Story

Two years ago, Monique assumed the leadership of a dynamic, successful team of trainers, a group highly regarded both within and outside their IT organization. Simultaneously with this leadership transition, substantial organizational policy and procedure changes began to be instituted by the organization's HR department and the departmental VP, a further source of anxiety for the team. However, since Monique herself had been a highly respected member of the team just two years before, they were encouraged to know that "one of their own" was coming back to lead them. The group was confident that the positive, warm, and fun-loving atmosphere that characterized their team would continue under her leadership.

Now, two years later, virtually every member of the team feels demoralized. Most have become quite cynical about the organization and are quietly seeking employment elsewhere. The trainers have lost confidence in Monique's leadership and have little respect for her.

Comments by her staff members reveal that the primary cause of discontent is the highly impersonal leadership approach that Monique demonstrates. Although she actually cares deeply for her staff, Monique's communication style is very matter-of-fact, direct, and lacking in warmth. Typically, she simply announces changes to the team as a "faits accomplis" without initiating discussion about the impact on team members or providing an explanation of the rationale behind the changes. She conveys the belief that people should just "get with the new program and quit complaining."

When several of her staff finally spoke to her about the impact of her communication and decision-making styles, Monique was quite surprised and confused. She was unaware of the harmful impact of the way she communicated with her staff members. Regrettably, she continues to demonstrate the very same behaviors—much to the continuing frustration of her staff. Monique's lack of self-awareness blinds her to the demoralizing impact of her communication and decision-making approaches. She remains unaware that there is a link between her actions and the low morale of her team.

Most relevant to the focus of this book is the importance of *being highly aware of your full complement of strengths.* The approach to leadership effectiveness we are describing is based on leveraging your strengths in ways that allow you to use the most appropriate Leadership Dimensions for the situation. You cannot leverage something you don't know you have!

Acquiring a thorough understanding of their strengths is a challenge for many leaders. In our experience, the majority of organizational executives are more action oriented than introspective. Thus, deep self-awareness may not come naturally. In fact, until recently, self-awareness has not been a major consideration in the business world.

The remainder of this chapter provides you with a process and tools for determining your primary leadership strengths. The process is rooted in a framework for self-understanding called the Johari Window, first developed in the 1950s by Joseph Luft and Harrington Ingram (see Figure 3).

The four panes of the Johari Window represent four aspects of self-knowledge.

Figure 3

THE JOHARI WINDOW: A FRAMEWORK FOR INCREASING SELF-AWARENESS

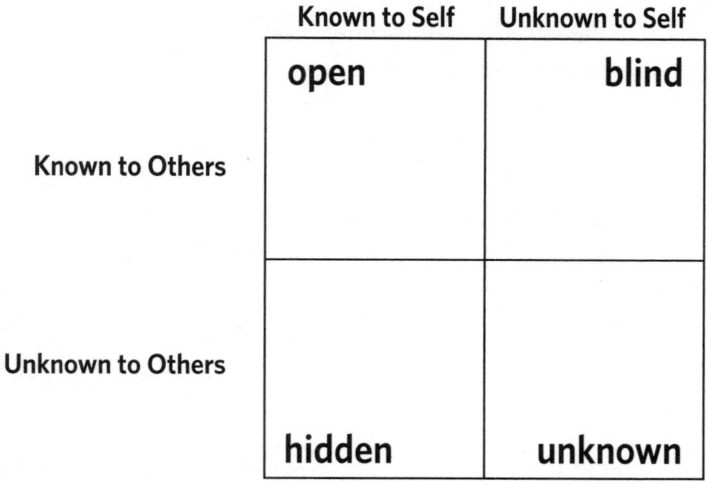

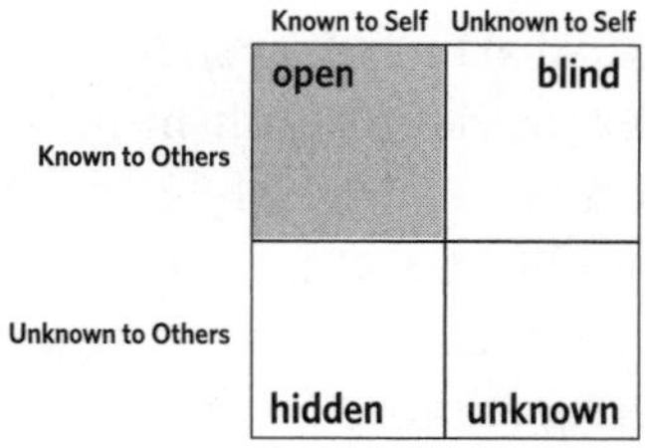

	Known to Self	Unknown to Self
Known to Others	open	blind
Unknown to Others	hidden	unknown

Open: The *open* quadrant includes those parts of yourself—for example, attitudes, behavior, motivation, way of life—of which you are aware and that you freely share and discuss with others.

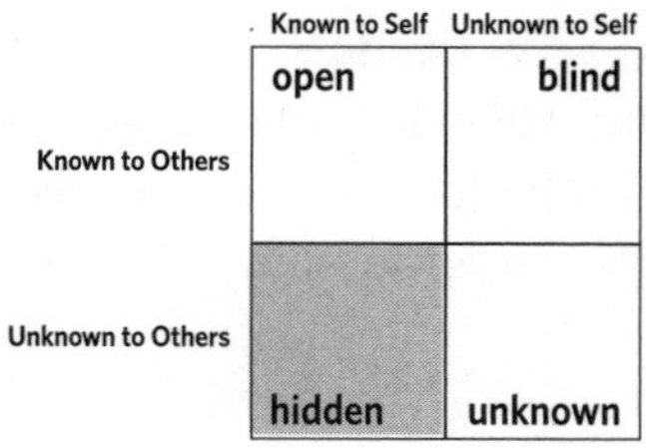

	Known to Self	Unknown to Self
Known to Others	open	blind
Unknown to Others	hidden	unknown

Hidden: The *hidden* quadrant contains things that you know about yourself but others do not unless you disclose them—things like your priorities, values, preferred way of getting information, decision-making style.

	Known to Self	Unknown to Self
Known to Others	open	blind
Unknown to Others	hidden	unknown

Blind: The *blind* quadrant encompasses the things about yourself that others see but of which you are unaware or that you imagine to be true when they are not (for example, strengths, characteristics, or mannerisms). It is critical to realize that we all have things about ourselves that we distort or to which we are blind.

	Known to Self	Unknown to Self
Known to Others	open	blind
Unknown to Others	hidden	unknown

Unknown: The fourth window represents the *unknown:* those aspects of which you and others are not aware, often referred to as the unconscious.

	Known to Self	Unknown to Self
Known to Others	open	blind
Unknown to Others	hidden	unknown

The Johari Window positions current levels of awareness both within and without, setting the stage for ways to increase your self-awareness and help others understand you better.

For example, at times your colleagues or direct reports may be perplexed about why you have responded to them as you have. Such confusion tends to result in misunderstanding, hurt feelings, conflict, or mistrust—all of which can rob your organization of productivity and your life of satisfaction. You may be aware of why you did what you did even if they are not. In other words, you are operating out of your hidden quadrant (things about yourself you know that others don't). By *disclosing* relevant personal information you move from the hidden quadrant into the open quadrant, as Figure 4 indicates. Sharing knowledge tends to improve your work relationships and increase your leadership effectiveness. The key is to disclose *appropriate* information—things that will help others work with you more effectively.

The Johari Window also suggests that you can increase your self-awareness—and thus your leadership effectiveness—by tapping into the

Figure 4
THE RESULTS OF DISCLOSURE

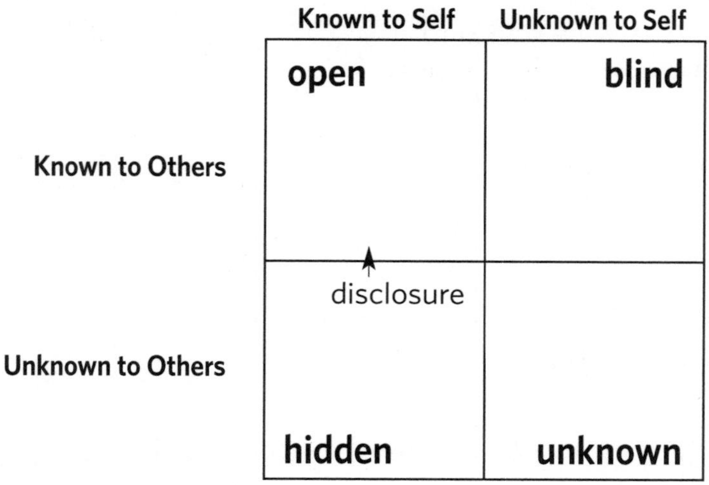

	Known to Self	Unknown to Self
Known to Others	open	blind
Unknown to Others	disclosure ↑	
	hidden	unknown

knowledge that others possess about you that you lack (the blind quadrant). *Feedback* is the mechanism by which you become aware of these aspects and develop a more accurate picture of yourself. When you receive this feedback, the information moves into the open quadrant (see Figure 5).

Finally, according to the Johari Window framework, there are likely aspects of yourself that currently lie outside your conscious awareness, in the unknown quadrant. Introspection, reflection, and interaction with others can often lead to *insight*, moving these aspects from the unknown quadrant to the hidden quadrant (see Figure 6). By going through the process in this chapter you will open the door for some of these personal revelations. Once you have this newly gained self-awareness, you can then decide what you want to disclose to others, moving those insights into the open quadrant.

Figure 5
THE RESULTS OF FEEDBACK

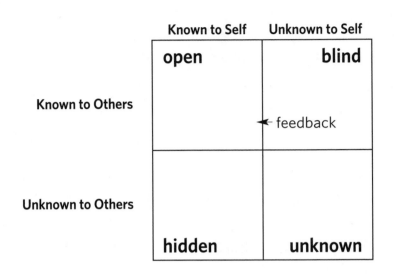

	Known to Self	Unknown to Self
Known to Others	open	blind ← feedback
Unknown to Others	hidden	unknown

Figure 6
THE RESULTS OF INSIGHT

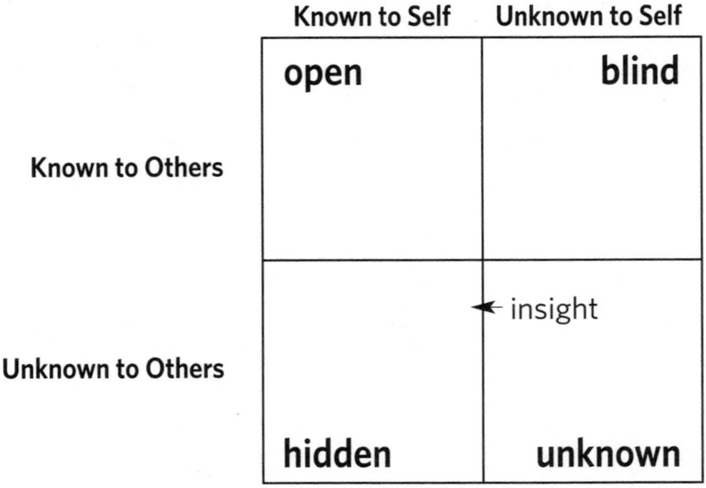

	Known to Self	Unknown to Self
Known to Others	open	blind
Unknown to Others	hidden	← insight unknown

Self-Awareness and Successful Change: Mark's Story

Mark is the CEO of an auto parts manufacturing firm in Michigan and a natural visionary leader. Due to increased competition from developing countries, Mark's company was forced to outsource a significant portion of their work to Mexico three years ago. They have also invested heavily in new technologies for their American plant, enabling them to increase speed of production while lowering costs. These changes, however, have also resulted in a 40% reduction in staff. Additionally, rumors of buyouts and mergers have circulated in the company for the past two years.

Remarkably, despite these dramatic changes and an atmosphere of uncertainty, Mark's direct reports and the vast majority of staff continue to demonstrate both a strong sense of loyalty to the company and cautious optimism about the future. This uncommon response is largely attributable to Mark's leadership during this stressful time of change. Mark's effectiveness is a direct outcome of his own deep self-awareness, an awareness enhanced by being open to feedback.

For example, Mark is by nature highly optimistic. His tendency is to downplay or ignore people's worries and fears. Mark became aware of this tendency through the candid feedback he received from two of his VPs. Rather than reacting defensively to this information, he has incorporated it into his leadership style. Consequently, during this recent time of stress and change, Mark has consciously used his listening skills to stay connected to his direct reports and numerous other staff. He has directly asked them to voice their concerns and worries, both one-on-one and at informal companywide gatherings. Rather than downplaying or belittling their apprehensions, Mark has used his skills to legitimize their feelings—a highly effective use of the Relating Leadership Dimension.

Mark also knows that information needs to be dispersed frequently during times of change. Thus, although he prefers face-to-face communication to writing memos and newsletters, he has motivated himself to send out biweekly updates from his office to all staff during the past three years. In these communiqués, he has again consciously drawn on his empathy to put himself in the place of his workforce and directly address their anxieties. While openly addressing the pain of the recent layoffs and the increased uncertainty of the climate in which they now operate, Mark has also used his natural Visioning Dimension to inspire confidence in the company's future success.

Mark's actions are rooted in a high degree of self-awareness about his strengths, enabling him to use them strategically and effectively in the midst of a swirl of change.

CREATING SELF-AWARENESS
A Leadership Strengths Checklist

Most Americans do not know what their strengths are. When you ask them, they look at you with a blank stare, or they respond in terms of subject knowledge, which is the wrong answer.

—*Peter F. Drucker, management consultant*

The first step in deepening your awareness of your leadership strengths is to complete the checklist in Tool 1. Think broadly about your leadership experiences as you do this exercise. You may not be using a particular strength in your present organizational role, but maybe you used it extensively in the past or use it frequently outside of work.

The purpose of this activity is to determine the strengths you already *possess*, not whether you are currently *using* them at work.

The Tool 1 checklist is extensive but not all-inclusive, so use it only as a launching point. You can record at the end of the checklist any additional strengths you possess that are not mentioned.

Tool 1

LEADERSHIP STRENGTHS CHECKLIST

Directions: Read each of the eighty-two items and decide which statements match one of your own strengths. Mark each of your personal strengths with a checkmark in the Step 1 column. Then go back over your list, and for each of the items you checked off as a strength, rate yourself from 1 to 3 in the Step 2 column: (1 = competent, 2 = superior, 3 = masterful).

Strength	Step 1	Step 2
1. I adapt what I have to the needs/ opportunities of the moment.	____	____
2. I am calm under pressure.	____	____
3. I confront problems quickly and directly.	____	____
4. I always meet my commitments.	____	____
5. I am disciplined and self-controlled.	____	____
6. I am proactive rather than reactive toward situations.	____	____
7. I am able to express emotions appropriately.	____	____
8. I keep disruptive emotions under control.	____	____
9. I am objective in analyzing problems and situations.	____	____
10. I am driven to achieve.	____	____
11. I marshal resources effectively to achieve objectives.	____	____
12. I am optimistic when facing problems or disappointments.	____	____
13. I make and keep a schedule.	____	____
14. I respond quickly to unexpected events.	____	____
15. I readily share my feelings.	____	____
16. I am willing to take risks.	____	____
17. I am able to calculate risks effectively.	____	____
18. I take the initiative.	____	____

continues ➜

Tool 1 cont'd

Strength	Step 1	Step 2
19. I am a catalyst for change.	____	____
20. I identify with and understand others' feelings.	____	____
21. I am emotionally self-aware.	____	____
22. I understand and work with the politics in my organization.	____	____
23. I accommodate others' needs, wants, and perspectives.	____	____
24. I am emotionally supportive of others.	____	____
25. I use my gut feelings to guide me.	____	____
26. I am confident in my decisions and abilities.	____	____
27. I offer meaningful praise and recognition to others.	____	____
28. I am able to get others to buy into ideas and plans.	____	____
29. I advise and guide others' career development.	____	____
30. I have animated gestures, facial expressions and tones of voice.	____	____
31. I am articulate in expressing ideas, concepts, or plans.	____	____
32. I inspire others to action or toward accomplishing a vision.	____	____
33. I clarify accurately the meaning of what others say or write.	____	____
34. I am able to build consensus.	____	____
35. I listen to understand others' meaning.	____	____
36. I use a collaborative approach to accomplishing tasks.	____	____
37. I am inclusive of other people, especially outsiders.	____	____

Strength	Step 1	Step 2
38. I delegate tasks effectively.	____	____
39. I am candid in communicating information.	____	____
40. I counsel others in ways that create a change in their behavior or beliefs.	____	____
41. I manage crises effectively.	____	____
42. I manage conflict between individuals or groups, arriving at lasting resolutions.	____	____
43. I tell stories for impact or clarifying meaning.	____	____
44. I am persuasive.	____	____
45. I provide for others' needs in practical ways.	____	____
46. I recognize and develop others' potential.	____	____
47. I recognize and seize opportunities.	____	____
48. I show tact and skill when dealing with people.	____	____
49. I negotiate mutually acceptable decisions.	____	____
50. I teach others how to do things effectively.	____	____
51. I unify a group.	____	____
52. I inspire others.	____	____
53. I build bonds with others easily.	____	____
54. I am able to create an effective team.	____	____
55. I set expectations.	____	____
56. I categorize information usefully.	____	____
57. I am able to anticipate the consequences of changes.	____	____
58. I conceptualize from particulars.	____	____
59. I organize the external environment for efficiency.	____	____
60. I design the form or structure of something in a way that makes it work effectively.	____	____
61. I have great factual recall.	____	____

continues →

Tool 1 cont'd

Strength	Step 1	Step 2
62. I envision clearly a desired result or future condition.	____	____
63. I plan an efficient series of steps.	____	____
64. I analyze problems practically.	____	____
65. I strategize to achieve goals effectively.	____	____
66. I seek the advice and expertise of others.	____	____
67. I am friendly.	____	____
68. I am enthusiastic.	____	____
69. I am intuitive.	____	____
70. I am innovative.	____	____
71. I see the big picture.	____	____
72. I am imaginative.	____	____
73. I am fun loving.	____	____
74. I am energetic.	____	____
75. I pay meticulous attention to detail.	____	____
76. I monitor the accuracy and efficiency of processes.	____	____
77. I use humor well.	____	____
78. I am achievement oriented.	____	____
79. I recognize the need for and make quick decisions.	____	____
80. I am people oriented.	____	____
81. I am visionary.	____	____
82. I am warmhearted.	____	____
_____	____	____
_____	____	____
_____	____	____
_____	____	____

SUMMARY OF LEADERSHIP STRENGTHS FROM THE CHECKLIST

Use this chart to record your most highly rated strengths, starting with the ones you rated as 3. (The chart allows for recording fifteen of them). You'll return to this later.

- _____
- _____
- _____
- _____
- _____
- _____
- _____
- _____
- _____
- _____
- _____
- _____
- _____
- _____
- _____

DEEPENING SELF-AWARENESS
Reviewing Past Leadership Successes

The definition of a strength . . . is quite specific:
consistent near perfect performance in an activity.

—Marcus Buckingham & Donald O. Clifton,
Now, Discover Your Strengths

A checklist is a helpful tool for initiating personal reflection. More useful still is an exploration of previous instances of successful leadership. Earlier we defined leadership as the process of achieving desired results through people. Here you will consider some examples of when you did this with great effectiveness.

Tool 2 will guide you to reflect on times when you have demonstrated leadership success. Don't feel your examples need to be recent or from your current organization. They might not be drawn from a work setting at all; they might arise from your involvement on the board of a charitable organization, your participation in a political campaign, or perhaps your leadership in a community association. The key is to look for specific examples of your success as a leader.

VALUING SELF-AWARENESS
The Foundation of Effective Leadership

CREATING SELF-AWARENESS
A Leadership Strengths Checklist

DEEPENING SELF-AWARENESS
Reviewing Past Leadership Successes

EXPANDING SELF-AWARENESS
Employing 360° Feedback

CONSOLIDATING SELF-AWARENESS
Your Strengths-at-a-Glance Chart

Tool 2

LEADERSHIP SUCCESS REVIEW

Directions: Recall times when you have demonstrated effective leadership. Answer questions about these success stories in the space provided.

For you to gain the benefits of reviewing your leadership successes, two things are required:

1. You need to consider a sufficient number of examples—we recommend a minimum of three.
2. You need to describe—with as much specificity as possible—the details of these occasions. You may need to ask a few trusted colleagues to remind you of some examples.

LEADERSHIP SUCCESS STORY #1

What were the circumstances of the situation? What was the problem? Who was involved? What was the outcome or result?

_____

_____

_____

_____

_____

Specifically, what did you do that was effective?

_____

_____

_____

_____

What strengths allowed you to be successful? It may be helpful to refer to the checklist in Tool 1 in considering the specific strengths you used.

_____

_____

_____

_____

_____

continues ➜

Tool 2 cont'd

LEADERSHIP SUCCESS STORY #2

What were the circumstances of the situation? What was the problem? Who was involved? What was the outcome or result?

_____

_____

_____

_____

_____

Specifically, what did you do that was effective?

_____

_____

_____

_____

What strengths allowed you to be successful? It may be helpful to refer to the checklist in Tool 1 in considering the specific strengths you used.

_____

_____

_____

_____

LEADERSHIP SUCCESS STORY #3

What were the circumstances of the situation? What was the problem?
Who was involved? What was the outcome or result?

_____

_____

_____

_____

_____

Specifically, what did you do that was effective?

_____

_____

_____

_____

What strengths allowed you to be successful? It may be helpful to refer
to the checklist in Tool 1 in considering the specific strengths you used.

_____

_____

_____

_____

_____

continues ➔

Tool 2 cont'd

LEADERSHIP SUCCESS STORY #4

What were the circumstances of the situation? What was the problem?
Who was involved? What was the outcome or result?

_____

_____

_____

_____

_____

Specifically, what did you do that was effective?

_____

_____

_____

_____

_____

What strengths allowed you to be successful? It may be helpful to refer
to the checklist in Tool 1 in considering the specific strengths you used.

_____

_____

_____

_____

_____

SUMMARY OF LEADERSHIP STRENGTHS FROM THE REVIEW

Now that you have considered these examples, some strengths may stand out as ones you have used regularly with great effectiveness. Alternatively, some of your greatest successes may have come from strengths you have used only infrequently. In either case, in the chart below, record the strengths you think have contributed the most to your past successes. Don't worry about terminology—define each strength in the way that makes the most sense to you.

_____

_____

_____

_____

_____

_____

_____

_____

_____

_____

_____

_____

_____

_____

_____

EXPANDING SELF-AWARENESS
Employing 360° Feedback

While managers can make an educated guess as to their success, employers and co-workers experience the reality.

—HumanR 2000

Obtaining pertinent feedback from others is one of the most powerful ways of increasing self-awareness.

People often regard feedback as a negative process, focusing largely on one's *weaknesses* and *development needs*. While negative information has some limited value, the 5-D Leadership emphasis is different.

Feedback can be one of the most helpful tools for gaining a reliable and comprehensive understanding of your *strengths*. Many of us are either unaware of or undervalue our primary strengths; feedback from others can help us see them.

VALUING SELF-AWARENESS
The Foundation of Effective Leadership

CREATING SELF-AWARENESS
A Leadership Strengths Checklist

DEEPENING SELF-AWARENESS
Reviewing Past Leadership Successes

EXPANDING SELF-AWARENESS
Employing 360° Feedback

CONSOLIDATING SELF-AWARENESS
Your Strengths-at-a-Glance Chart

The use of "360° feedback" in organizations has been growing steadily during the past decade. It has demonstrated itself to be useful for developing performance at all levels of the organization. The term *360° feedback* uses the metaphor of a compass, as shown in Figure 7, and suggests that for feedback to be most helpful, it should come from a variety of sources. Get feedback not only from your manager but also from colleagues and direct reports for a fuller, more accurate picture of your actual strengths. It can also be helpful to ask for feedback from former colleagues and subordinates, especially if your leadership context has changed recently. Particular attention should be paid to those who most directly experience your leadership—your direct reports.

It takes humility to seek feedback. It takes wisdom to understand it, analyze it, and appropriately act on it.
—Stephen R. Covey,
First Things First

Figure 7
THE DYNAMICS OF 360° FEEDBACK

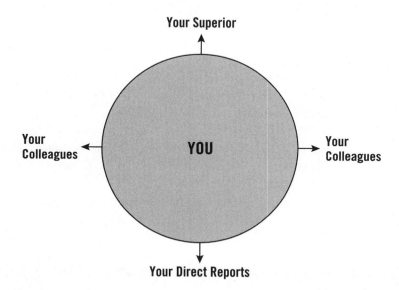

For the process of 360° feedback to be most effective, it is best to follow these guidelines:

1. Make sure you select people who know your leadership practices well enough to be able to assess your strengths reliably.

2. Ask a sufficient number of people to enable you to see trends and rule out aberrations (we recommend at least two colleagues/peers and four direct reports). You may want to ask for feedback by saying something like, "I read this really great book about leadership and it recommended asking several people about my leadership strengths to get more perspective. I was wondering if you would take ten to fifteen minutes to complete this form and get it back to me by _____. As this is for my information only, I would really appreciate your being candid in your responses."

3. If you think people will be concerned about giving a written record of their comments, you may want to ask for their verbal feedback instead. Assure them that this is for your personal use only and that their comments will not be mentioned to anyone else. Make sure you keep your word!

4. Don't enlist just people who will tell you what they think you want to hear; ask people who will be *honest*.

Use the chart in Tool 3 to write out the names of those who you think can provide you with the most helpful feedback.

To facilitate this 360° feedback process, use the reproducible form in Tool 4 to give to people you've asked to give you feedback. This form is also available as a downloadable PDF file on our web site: www.5DLeadership.com.

Make sure you write a return date in the top line, as people tend to respond more promptly if there is a specific deadline.

Tool 3

INDIVIDUALS TO ASK FOR FEEDBACK REGARDING MY LEADERSHIP STRENGTHS

Name	Working Relationship (boss, colleague, direct report)
_____	_____
_____	_____
_____	_____
_____	_____
_____	_____
_____	_____
_____	_____

Tool 4

360° FEEDBACK FORM

To _____ **Return by** _____

Directions: Please take a few minutes to complete this form and return it to me by the date shown above. This is for my information only, so I would appreciate your being as candid as possible.

1. As a leader, what things do I do best?

2. As a leader, what are my best personal attributes (characteristics)?

3. Rank my effectiveness in the five Leadership Dimensions described below. The one you rank as #1 is the response that you think I am best at; #5 is the one at which I am weakest.

Leadership Dimension		**Ranking**
Commanding	Taking charge and seeking immediate compliance to quickly effect a desired result	_____
Visioning	Creating and effectively communicating a clear and compelling picture of a worthwhile future for the group	_____
Enrolling	Creating buy-in and commitment by genuinely seeking input or employing democratic decision-making processes, or both	_____
Relating	Creating and sustaining harmonious relationships (1) between myself and individual staff members, and (2) among my staff members themselves	_____
Coaching	Developing an individual's potential and performance while aligning the individual's goals and values with those of the organization	_____

continues ➡

Tool 4 cont'd

SUMMARY OF LEADERSHIP STRENGTHS FROM THE 360° FEEDBACK

After you have reviewed your 360° feedback forms, you can list the strengths most frequently mentioned.

- _____
- _____
- _____
- _____
- _____
- _____
- _____
- _____
- _____
- _____
- _____
- _____
- _____
- _____
- _____
- _____
- _____
- _____
- _____

If you have completed the prior steps in this chapter, it is likely that you feel pleased with your new level of awareness regarding your personal leadership strengths. If you feel the need for further insight into your strengths, there are several additional formal assessment tools that may be beneficial. See Appendix C for recommendations.

CONSOLIDATING SELF-AWARENESS
Your Strengths at a Glance Chart

The chart in Tool 5 is one you will return to several times as you work through the rest of the book. It provides a convenient summary of your primary leadership strengths. These strengths are the key to effectively using the relevant Leadership Dimension(s) for your context. Knowing your strengths will also help you determine *your natural Leadership Dimensions*, a topic we will explore in the next chapter.

VALUING SELF-AWARENESS
The Foundation of Effective Leadership

CREATING SELF-AWARENESS
A Leadership Strengths Checklist

DEEPENING SELF-AWARENESS
Reviewing Past Leadership Successes

EXPANDING SELF-AWARENESS
Employing 360° Feedback

CONSOLIDATING SELF-AWARENESS
Your Strengths-at-a-Glance Chart

Take a few minutes now to complete the chart before continuing your reading. Even if you are planning to complete one or more formal assessment tools such as those listed in Appendix C, we encourage you to draft a preliminary summary of your strengths based on your current degree of insight. If need be, you can revise it after completing the assessment instruments.

CONCLUSION

Now that you have a much deeper awareness of your unique leadership *strengths*, let's take a look at the next chapter for ways to identify your natural Leadership Dimensions.

Tool 5

MY STRENGTHS AT A GLANCE

Directions: Use these three steps to complete your Strengths at a Glance chart.

1. Review the leadership strengths summary charts on pages 105, 111, and 116. As you look over these three lists, try to determine which strengths are your principal ones. Note especially any strengths that occur in all three charts.
2. Write your top twelve strengths in the left-hand column of the Strengths at a Glance chart. Feel free to use your own terminology for these and list them in rough order, from the most developed to the least.
3. Specify in the right-hand column the typical results achieved when you have used this strength. For example, if your sense of humor is one of your strengths, consider whether it usually functions as a tension breaker in conflict situations, a morale booster when people are bored or discouraged, or a way of helping people manage their stress in the midst of busy, demanding circumstances.

Personal Leadership Strengths

Typical Results of Using This Strength

1.
2.
3.
4.
5.
6.
7.
8.
9.
10.
11.
12.

CHAPTER **6**

IDENTIFY YOUR LEADERSHIP DIMENSIONS

TOOLS FOR SELF-DISCOVERY

Until you make your life your own, you're walking around in borrowed clothes. Leaders, whatever their field, are made up as much of their experiences as their skills, like everyone else. Unlike everyone else, they use their experience rather than being used by it.

—*Warren Bennis*

Exploring your natural strengths and innate abilities has prepared you for the next step: you are ready to discover which of the five Leadership Dimensions are natural to you and which will require the most conscious development and use. This chapter will provide you with the tools to do that.

Just as you have a unique mix of natural strengths, most individuals possess the natural beliefs, values, and skills associated with one or more of the five Dimensions. In our experience, everyone naturally prefers at least one of the five Dimensions, and most people have a natural affinity for two. A much smaller number seem to connect naturally to three.

A few individuals in history seem to have moved naturally between four of the Dimensions (Shackleton, for example), but we are still waiting to meet someone who naturally has all five! The point is that some of these Dimensions will always be easier and more instinctive to you than others, and you shouldn't panic if you possess only one Dimension naturally. In this book, you've learned that you can develop *effectiveness* in all five, even if you are never fully comfortable with some of them.

It's wise to know which of these dimensions are your home base (so you can use them as often as possible and maximize both your effectiveness and your enjoyment) and which will require more conscious use (requiring you to leverage your strengths into behaviors that may not be natural for you).

Before beginning this self-discovery process, beware of making two false assumptions:

- Don't assume that your experience alone indicates your natural Leadership Dimensions.

- Don't assume that a preference for a Dimension automatically means a high degree of skill in that Dimension.

You'll see why as you read through this chapter.

It is very important to go through the process laid out in this chapter before reaching a conclusion about your natural Leadership Dimensions because it is entirely possible that you have used one or more of them only on rare occasions in your professional leadership role and thus may not recognize them. The infrequent or complete disuse of natural Dimensions is often the result of having adopted (consciously or unconsciously) another person's leadership style as your model. You may have experienced excellent leadership from a former manager and assumed that what worked for that person should work for you. Unfortunately, this shortcut ignores the importance of adapting your own Leadership Dimensions to your particular leadership context; it overlooks the effectiveness that comes from being yourself, not an imitation of someone else, and, most important, it doesn't let you capitalize on your natural strengths.

Another common reason why individuals have not used their natural Leadership Dimensions is organizational or managerial sanction. In some organizations (or perhaps with a particular manager), certain Leadership Dimensions are approved and others proscribed, either directly or indirectly.

For example, one company we worked with had an organizational culture (established by its founder) that permitted only the Relating and Enrolling Dimensions. Though this was never stated, it clearly operated through all levels of leadership in the company. Managers who tried to coach their staff were reprimanded for not "trusting their people" and "micromanaging." Needless to say, Commanding someone (even in cases of highly inappropriate behavior by a staff member) was outlawed. When we first started working with them, it was a case of the inmates running the asylum. There was no unifying vision and little consequence for poor performance. It took a great deal of work to shift the culture to one that incorporated accountability, performance management, and a clear sense of direction. In this setting, numerous leaders never had the opportunity to use their natural Coaching, Visioning, or Commanding Dimensions, approaches that could have strengthened the organization. It is possible that you have been in a similar setting where one or more of the Leadership Dimensions are discouraged or forbidden —perhaps the very ones that are natural to you.

The point is worth repeating: *Don't assume that your experience alone indicates your natural Leadership Dimensions.*

The second caution is also worth repeating: *Don't assume that a preference for a dimension automatically means a high degree of skill in that dimension,* particularly if you have not had much opportunity to use it.

However, a natural preference for a particular Dimension *does* suggest that becoming highly skilled in its use will happen quickly, with relative ease and minimal blunders! This is where your strongest leverage applies in developing leadership effectiveness. When you can draw on your natural values, beliefs, and strengths, learning is fast, powerful, and lasting.

With these perspectives in mind, let's begin the process of determining your natural Leadership Dimensions.

MINDING YOUR MUSINGS
Assessing Your Characteristics and Behaviors

Honesty is the first chapter of the book of wisdom.

—*Thomas Jefferson*

Keeping in mind the cautions about assuming too much from your past leadership experiences, those experiences are, nonetheless, a natural place to begin. Many individuals *have* had the opportunity to use their natural Dimensions (often without knowing that they were doing so). The Characteristics and Beliefs Checklist, Tool 6, will enable you to assess your past leadership experiences. Be sure to consider not only your *formal* leadership responsibilities but also *ad hoc* leadership opportunities you have had at work and the leadership roles you have played in your family, community, or associations.

As Thomas Jefferson pointed out, wisdom begins with honesty, so try to select answers based on what is actually true of you, not what you wish were true. The checklist is divided into five lists, one for each of the five Leadership Dimensions.

In completing Tool 6, you will have taken the first step in appraising your natural Leadership Dimensions. However, if you have some significant gaps in your experience or you have had limited opportunities to actually do what comes naturally to you, the ranking in Tool 6 may not be accurate. So let's move to the next self-assessment tool.

MAPPING YOUR MIND
Exploring Your Leadership Beliefs

People seem not to see that their opinion of the world is also a confession of their character.

—*Ralph Waldo Emerson*

Everyone has some beliefs that are natural to them emerging from their personal values and priorities. Frequently, these beliefs correspond with certain of the five Leadership Dimensions. Consequently, exploring your

Tool 6

CHARACTERISTICS AND BEHAVIORS CHECKLIST

Directions: Based on your past leadership experiences, consider each item in the left column separately and decide if it is always true of you, somewhat true, or not at all true of you. Place a checkmark in the appropriate column to the right. Then tally up your total checkmarks for the three columns for each of the Leadership Dimensions.

COMMANDING DIMENSION

Statement	Always True of Me	Somewhat True of Me	Not At All True of Me
I face adversity head-on.	☐	☐	☐
I am comfortable making decisions and acting without having all the information.	☐	☐	☐
I am comfortable handling risk.	☐	☐	☐
I am cool under pressure.	☐	☐	☐
I am able to quickly make decisions that will directly affect others.	☐	☐	☐
I am energized by tough challenges.	☐	☐	☐
I am comfortable taking unpopular stands if necessary.	☐	☐	☐
I deal with problematic direct reports firmly and enforce consequences if they refuse to comply.	☐	☐	☐
I delegate tasks clearly and comfortably.	☐	☐	☐
I determine priorities quickly and accurately in a crisis.	☐	☐	☐
I encourage direct and tough debate but I'm not afraid to end it when I've heard enough.	☐	☐	☐
I monitor compliance to objectives and results and am comfortable holding people accountable.	☐	☐	☐
Total Number of Checkmarks	____	____	____

continues ➝

Tool 6 cont'd

VISIONING DIMENSION

Statement	Always True of Me	Somewhat True of Me	Not At All True of Me
I understand future implications of current trends.	☐	☐	☐
I verbally and articulately paint credible pictures of future possibilities.	☐	☐	☐
I talk about the future frequently.	☐	☐	☐
I am optimistic about the future.	☐	☐	☐
I can relate my picture of the future to others' motivations and aspirations.	☐	☐	☐
I talk frequently about possibilities.	☐	☐	☐
I create symbols and mileposts to rally people behind the vision.	☐	☐	☐
I publicly recognize steps taken by people to realize the vision.	☐	☐	☐
I align systems and processes to support the desired future.	☐	☐	☐
I encourage people to act in new ways and support them if they fail.	☐	☐	☐
I act in ways that are consistent with my vision of the future.	☐	☐	☐
I communicate the vision frequently using a wide variety of means.	☐	☐	☐
Total Number of Checkmarks	_____	_____	_____

ENROLLING DIMENSION

Statement	Always True of Me	Somewhat True of Me	Not At All True of Me
I genuinely believe others have valuable insights and ideas to offer.	☐	☐	☐
I respond to others' suggestions with respect and curiosity.	☐	☐	☐
I am comfortable admitting that I need others input in decision making.	☐	☐	☐
I regularly ask for others' ideas and insights.	☐	☐	☐
I am patient with group processes of brainstorming and consensus building.	☐	☐	☐
I evaluate others' ideas fairly based on the merits of the idea, not the person proposing it.	☐	☐	☐
I provide meaningful recognition for others' contributions.	☐	☐	☐
I am effective at helping a group reach consensus, with excellent ideas emerging from the process.	☐	☐	☐
I respond calmly and openly when people tell me things with which I disagree.	☐	☐	☐
I build rapport and trust quickly in a group of people who are unfamiliar with one another.	☐	☐	☐
I regularly use the ideas of others, not just my own, and give credit for them.	☐	☐	☐
I am comfortable with conflict in a group and know how to use it to create consensus.	☐	☐	☐
Total Number of Checkmarks	____	____	____

continues →

Tool 6 cont'd

RELATING DIMENSION

Statement	Always True of Me	Somewhat True of Me	Not At All True of Me
I am genuinely interested in the work and personal lives of my direct reports.	☐	☐	☐
I am easy to approach and talk to.	☐	☐	☐
I am available to listen to personal problems and my direct reports regularly confide in me.	☐	☐	☐
I listen to others empathetically, making sure I truly understand the other's point of view.	☐	☐	☐
I am diplomatic and tactful.	☐	☐	☐
I can find common ground with those with whom I am in conflict and achieve win-win resolutions.	☐	☐	☐
I demonstrate real empathy with the joys and pains of others.	☐	☐	☐
I am easy to get to know.	☐	☐	☐
I regularly spend time with staff in informal conversations.	☐	☐	☐
I am effective in mediating conflicts between my direct reports, leading to win-win resolutions.	☐	☐	☐
I accurately restate the opinions and emotions of others even when I disagree.	☐	☐	☐
I create a strong sense of unity and mutual commitment in teams I lead.	☐	☐	☐
Total Number of Checkmarks	____	____	____

COACHING DIMENSION

Statement	Always True of Me	Somewhat True of Me	Not At All True of Me
I am highly aware of the unique motivations, values, talents, and interests of my direct reports.	☐	☐	☐
I care deeply about others achieving their potential.	☐	☐	☐
I provide appropriate stretch assignments that focus on developing my direct reports' strengths.	☐	☐	☐
I regularly review my direct reports' performance, providing timely and effective feedback.	☐	☐	☐
I am aware of each of my direct reports' career goals and aspirations.	☐	☐	☐
I easily and accurately identify others' natural strengths and potential.	☐	☐	☐
I enjoy working with people who need development.	☐	☐	☐
I naturally tune into others' motivations, values, and aspirations.	☐	☐	☐
I am able to relate a direct report's motivations and strengths to organizational goals and activities.	☐	☐	☐
I provide training/instruction that is geared to the individual and results in effective learning.	☐	☐	☐
I hold frequent developmental discussions (formal and informal) with direct reports.	☐	☐	☐
I am usually able to get a person to correct inappropriate behavior or poor performance.	☐	☐	☐
Total Number of Checkmarks	____	____	____

continues ➜

Tool 6 cont'd

SCORING THE CHARACTERISTICS AND BEHAVIORS CHECKLIST

Now that you have completed the checklist, you can use the scoring grid below to rank the five Dimensions. To calculate your scores, you will need to refer to the "Total Number of Checkmarks" row for each of the five Dimensions. First, for each of the Dimensions, take your "Always True of Me" total, multiply it by two, and enter that number in the appropriate space below. Second, transfer your actual totals from the "Somewhat True of Me" column to the appropriate space below. Third, add together the two scores below for each Dimension and record the total in the "Total Score" column on the right.

	Always True of Me Score x 2	Somewhat True of Me Score	Total Score
Commanding	____	____	____
Visioning	____	____	____
Enrolling	____	____	____
Relating	____	____	____
Coaching	____	____	____

Finally, rank the Dimensions below from highest score to lowest. In cases of a tie, record the Dimensions on the same line.

1. _____

2. _____

3. _____

4. _____

5. _____

true beliefs is another avenue you can use to determine which of the five Leadership Dimensions are most natural to you. As you complete Tool 7, it is important for you to be as honest with yourself as possible concerning what you most deeply believe, not what you think you "should" believe.

The Beliefs Survey (Tool 7) is the second tool to help you identify which of these five dimensions are most natural for you. The order in which the Leadership Dimensions are ranked may be similar to or quite different from that of the Characteristics and Behaviors Checklist (Tool 6). Consequently, there is one final assessment for you to complete to help solidify your awareness of your natural Leadership Dimensions.

PONDERING YOUR PROCLIVITIES
Analyzing Your Instinctive Responses

The leadership instinct you are born with is the backbone. You develop the funny bone and the wishbone that go with it.

—Elaine Agather

The final assessment tool for determining your natural Leadership Dimensions, Tool 8 (page 133), involves analyzing your innate preferences in responding to four hypothetical leadership scenarios. For this assessment to be most useful for you, focus on what you would *initially* be inclined to do, not necessarily what you would ultimately *choose* to do—your instinctive response, not your eventual behavior.

Tool 7

BELIEFS SURVEY

Directions: For each of the statements below, give yourself a score between 1 and 5, rating as follows:

1 = disagree strongly with the statement
2 = disagree somewhat with the statement
3 = am neutral or undecided toward the statement
4 = agree somewhat with the statement
5 = agree strongly with the statement

Belief	**Score 1—5**
1. People have a wealth of ideas to offer.	_____
2. People don't do what you expect, only what you inspect.	_____
3. People don't care how much you know until they know you really care.	_____
4. People support only what they create.	_____
5. People who share a vision will conquer any obstacle.	_____
6. People develop best by experimenting, taking risks, and learning from their mistakes.	_____
7. No matter what else you accomplish, if your people don't know you care about them, you've failed.	_____
8. The key to being a great leader is recognizing and developing others' talents.	_____
9. The key to being a great leader is admitting that you don't have all the answers—and that your people often do.	_____
10. The key to being a great leader is creating a vision for the future and the strategies for getting there.	_____
11. The key to being a great leader is acting decisively in order to get the job done.	_____
12. The leader's top priority is getting others to participate in making a difference.	_____
13. The growth and development of people is the highest calling of leadership.	_____

Belief	Score 1—5
14. The well-being of people is the leader's first priority.	_____
15. The very essence of leadership is that you have a clear and compelling vision of the future.	_____
16. Creating a sense of community and belonging is the leader's number one priority.	_____
17. Leaders can't afford to get too close to their people; familiarity breeds contempt.	_____
18. Leaders fail when they fail to inspire hope for the future.	_____
19. When staff members fail to perform, it is a sign that the leader has failed to teach them how to succeed.	_____
20. In truth, most people want someone to just tell them what to do.	_____
21. Leaders do what they must to align the organization's structures and values to their picture of the future.	_____
22. The main reason people leave a company is that they don't feel their manager cares for them as a person.	_____
23. It's better to act and be wrong than to fail to act and miss an opportunity.	_____
24. The opportunity to develop one's natural talents is one of the most powerful motivators at work and a major factor in retaining good people.	_____
25. Decisions made by all of us are better than the best decision made by the best one of us.	_____

continues →

Tool 7 cont'd

SCORING THE BELIEFS SURVEY

Transfer your scores to the table below and then total them in the right-hand column.

Commanding	Item 2	Item 11	Item 17	Item 20	Item 23	Total
Visioning	Item 5	Item 10	Item 15	Item 18	Item 21	Total
Enrolling	Item 1	Item 4	Item 9	Item 12	Item 25	Total
Relating	Item 3	Item 7	Item 14	Item 16	Item 22	Total
Coaching	Item 6	Item 8	Item 13	Item 19	Item 24	Total

Next, rank the dimensions from highest score to lowest. In cases of a tie, record the dimensions on the same line.

1. _____

2. _____

3. _____

4. _____

5. _____

SUMMARIZING YOUR DISCOVERIES
Charting Your Leadership Dimensions

I want, by understanding myself, to understand others.
I want to be all that I am capable of becoming.

—*Katherine Mansfield*

By now, you are probably gaining clarity regarding which Leadership Dimension or Dimensions are naturally yours. The Leadership Dimensions at a Glance chart in Tool 9 (page 139) gives you the opportunity to summarize your discoveries from this chapter about your natural leadership preferences.

Tool 8

INSTINCTIVE RESPONSES

Directions: Begin by reading scenarios 1 through 4 and recording your instinctive response to each in the space provided. ***Don't edit yourself or worry about the consequences of acting on your initial reaction.*** Simply record your first instinctive response.

Scenario 1

You are the leader of your company's elite account management team. This is a group of sales professionals who manage your organization's largest client accounts. You have become increasingly concerned that the performance level of one of your team members has seriously declined in the past three months. Reports are being turned in late to you. In the past week, two very important clients have complained that this account manager has been late for meetings, been tardy returning phone calls, and failed to keep them informed on the progress of several major acquisitions. Furthermore, this person has not landed a single new account during the past three months. Previously one of your top performers, this account manager has now become a serious concern for you and the company.

What is your instinctive response? What would you naturally be inclined to do?

_____

_____

_____

_____

_____

_____

_____

_____

continues ➜

Tool 8 cont'd

Scenario 2

You are the VP for marketing in your company. Your organization recently completed a buy-out of a smaller company. The buy-out was undertaken to try to bring some fresh perspectives and vitality into your company, as it has recently started to lose some of its market share. The composition of your division is now two-thirds members from your company and one-third members from the recently acquired company. The two companies had very different corporate cultures at the time of the buy-out. Your organization prided itself on (1) a long history as a leader in its industry and (2) its reputation for quality and service. Before the buy-out it had a very hierarchical leadership structure. The smaller company was known for its forward thinking and innovation and had a very relaxed, informal leadership structure. A significant minority of your original staff members are feeling somewhat resentful toward the newcomers. Some of the newcomers are wondering if they will eventually be let go; others have a bit of a messiah complex, thinking they are going to be the saviors of your organization. You need to find a way to bring these two cultures and groups together and use the strengths of both.

What is your instinctive response? What would you naturally be inclined to do?

_____

_____

_____

_____

_____

_____

IDENTIFY YOUR LEADERSHIP DIMENSIONS **135**

Scenario 3

You have just been promoted to CEO of a midsize manufacturing firm (fifteen hundred employees, four separate production facilities). There are five VPs on your executive team, all of whom have been with the company for at least five years. Your previous position was VP of finance, so you are intimately acquainted with the financial history of the organization, which includes a twenty-year history of consistent growth. During the past three years, however, profits have declined significantly. While there seemingly is no immediate crisis, there are grounds for serious concern. Your perception of the causes for this slowdown focuses on two issues: (1) aging and outdated technologies being used by your company, and (2) lower prices offered by the competition, who have relocated their production plants to less expensive overseas locations.

What is your instinctive response? What would you naturally be inclined to do?

_____

_____

_____

_____

_____

_____

_____

continues ➡

Tool 8 cont'd

Scenario 4

You are the leader of a small division of software developers. The company has been in existence for seven years and has been experiencing remarkable growth for the past two. Your team has grown quickly during those two years, expanding from seven developers to its current level of twenty-three. Approximately three-quarters of your people are under thirty years of age. For the past nine months growth has been incredibly robust, requiring everyone to work at full tilt—long hours, lots of weekends worked, no holidays. While there has been a strong sense of commitment and enthusiasm from your staff, signs of fatigue are now starting to show: tempers have been flaring, sick days have been increasing, and projects seem to be taking longer to complete, with more bugs in the software having to be fixed.

What is your instinctive response? What would you naturally be inclined to do?

_____

_____

_____

_____

_____

_____

_____

SUMMARY OF INSTINCTIVE RESPONSES

Now that you have recorded your initial responses to these four scenarios, go back to each and try to determine which Leadership Dimension, or combination of Dimensions, your instinctive response represents. Record your analysis.

Scenario 1   **Leadership Dimension(s) Indicated by My Response**

- _____

- _____

- _____

Scenario 2

- _____

- _____

- _____

Scenario 3

- _____

- _____

- _____

Scenario 4

- _____

- _____

- _____

continues →

Tool 8 cont'd

SUMMARY OF INSTINCTIVE RESPONSES

Do you see any trends in terms of naturally preferred dimensions? It's likely you will find that one or two of these dimensions show up frequently as instinctive responses and indicate your naturally preferred Leadership Dimensions. If so, rank and record them below.

1. _____

2. _____

3. _____

ASSESSING YOUR ALIGNMENT
Congruency and Leadership Effectiveness

A happy life is one which is in accordance with its own nature.

—*Marcus Annaeus Seneca*

How do you know when your automobile's wheels are out of alignment? The usual signal is the vibration in the steering wheel. Typically, the faster you go, the greater the vibration. If the misalignment is bad enough, and your speed is great enough, you become an accident waiting to happen.

The same can be said for leaders who fail to align either their natural Leadership Dimensions or their specific natural strengths with their circumstances. The key to creating alignment is awareness of your innate strengths and Leadership Dimensions. Self-knowledge allows you to fine-tune the alignment—making for a smoother ride for everyone concerned.

We are never happier than when we act in accordance with our nature. Knowing which of the five Dimensions are natural to you allows you to better choose environments—the organizational or departmental

Tool 9

MY LEADERSHIP DIMENSIONS AT A GLANCE

Characteristics and Behaviors Checklist Results
(Transfer results from Tool 6, p. 128)

1. _____

2. _____

3. _____

4. _____

5. _____

Beliefs Survey Results
(Transfer results from Tool 7, p. 132)

1. _____

2. _____

3. _____

4. _____

5. _____

Instinctive Responses Results
(Transfer results from Tool 8, p. 138)

1. _____

2. _____

3. _____

Ranking My Leadership Dimensions
(Based on the trends in your results of the three assessments in this chapter, rank your Leadership Dimensions from most natural to least natural.)

1. _____

2. _____

3. _____

4. _____

5. _____

culture and your specific responsibilities—that permit you to use these Dimensions as frequently as possible, maximizing your effectiveness and enjoyment and minimizing your stress.

Knowing your natural Dimensions also alerts you to situations where you will need to be more conscious of leveraging your strengths. If you find you are in a context that requires a Dimension particularly foreign to your nature, you will need to be quite deliberate in determining which of your unique personal strengths you can leverage in the situation to increase your effectiveness.

CONCLUSION

This chapter has provided you with the tools to determine which of the five Leadership Dimensions are most natural to you. Next you will determine which Dimensions you most need to be using in your context. In Part 3 we will explore the challenges and means of clearly seeing your context (Chapter 7) and the seven most common business contexts leaders encounter (Chapter 8).

PART 3

IDENTIFYING CONTEXTUAL DYNAMICS

Lasting leadership effectiveness requires the ability to *shift* between Leadership Dimensions in order to match the demands of the immediate business context. Now that you have determined your primary leadership strengths and your natural Leadership Dimensions, we'll turn to understanding the context in which you are leading. The dynamics of your business context determine which Leadership Dimension needs to be employed.

Chapter 7 will explore two common sources of misperception leaders face when trying to assess their context, and practical strategies for overcoming these sources of misperception.

Chapter 8 will provide an overview of seven common business contexts and their appropriate Leadership Dimensions. The chapter will conclude with a tool for helping you determine which of these seven contexts apply to your setting.

WHAT COLOR ARE YOUR GLASSES?

PERCEPTION ISN'T ALWAYS REALITY

People only see what they are prepared to see.
—Ralph Waldo Emerson

Wearing tinted sunglasses helps reduce the brightness of the sunlight, but an attendant effect is that we end up seeing the world in a distorted version of its true color. Yet even when we take off physical sunglasses, we continue to wear cognitive glasses—perceptual filters. These filters have a profound impact on how we perceive reality. In this chapter we will explore how, as a leader, your filters influence your perception of business situations.

Why does this matter?

You cannot choose the appropriate Leadership Dimension without assessing the situation. Your assessment is strongly influenced by your perceptual filters. The purpose of this chapter is to help you be aware of and overcome two key filters that affect your ability to assess your context accurately. Let's begin with a look at how your perceptual filters influence your perception of reality and the impact that has on your leadership effectiveness.

THE COSTS OF MISPERCEPTION

The French people are incapable of regicide.
—Louis XVI, king of France, 1789

I don't need bodyguards.
—Jimmy Hoffa

Misperceptions of reality are common—and often costly.

Chances are, you have already read the text inside the triangle in Figure 8. What does it say? If you are like the vast majority of people who have seen this diagram, you probably saw "A bird in the bush." If so, go back and look more carefully. You will see it actually says, "A bird in *the the* bush."

Figure 8
WHAT DOES IT SAY?

Misperceptions are often costly. Misperception cost both King Louis XVI and Jimmy Hoffa their lives. Granted it rarely leads to physical death in the business world, but misperceiving reality can be dangerous. Examples of this abound. Consider IBM, the giant of the mainframe computer business. In the 1980s, IBM's leaders believed that the emergence of minicomputers, microcomputers, and supercomputers was an insignificant development. That misperception nearly caused the company's demise. Or consider the North American automobile manufacturing industry. In the 1970s, the Big Three misperceived the change in customer values and priorities and quickly lost ground to the Japanese, whose automobiles tapped into customer desire for economy, quality, and longevity. That misperception cost the industry millions and millions of dollars. There are many such examples that could be detailed:

- Digital Equipment Corporation's misperception of the importance of personal computers and its consequent late entry into the field, ultimately leading to its demise[1]

- Coca-Cola's initial failure to see the potential of sports drinks (in contrast to Pepsi, which did see this opportunity and gained a huge market share advantage)

- Western Union's miscalculation of the potential of Alexander Graham Bell's telephone technology (Western Union's then president, William Orton, was offered the opportunity to buy Bell's telephone patent for $100,000 but turned down the offer. A report from a committee set up to investigate the offer referred to the invention as "hardly more than a toy.")[2]

- The near collapse of the Swiss watchmaking industry in the 1970s due to its stunning failure to see the value of *its own invention*— quartz timekeeping technology (the very technology Seiko used to obtain market dominance in that decade)

The costs of misperception by leaders are not usually as threatening to a business as in the examples cited above. But they can still be significant. These include the negative effects that typically ensue when leaders misperceive their circumstances and respond with Leadership Dimensions that are inappropriate to the context.

A list of these effects would include

- Lack of commitment from employees

- Low levels of worker productivity

- Needless management-labor conflict

- Failure to retain top talent

- Undeveloped leadership potential

- Missed opportunities to improve quality, save money, and delight customers

- Failure to take advantage of new business opportunities

These costs may not topple a business, but they can keep it from achieving its actual potential.

Obviously, the converse is also true. When leaders are able to perceive reality accurately, it is much easier to choose the most appropriate Leadership Dimension (or combination of Dimensions) with which to respond, thereby increasing their leverage.

EVERYBODY WEARS GLASSES
Perception, Interpretation, and Reality

People's behavior and judgment is based on their perception, they don't see reality itself. They interpret what they see and call it reality.

—*Rahim Poonjani,* From Perception to Reality

It is hard for some to admit, yet the truth is that *no one sees reality completely as it is.* Some individuals may perceive reality more fully than others, but no one sees a situation with total accuracy. Frequently, when we disagree with others' perceptions of an event or set of circumstances, we assume that we are right and they are wrong. Of course, they assume the same—they're right and we're wrong—often leading to intractable arguments in which we try to convince them of their faulty views. In most cases, we are actually each seeing a valid *aspect* of the reality facing us, not the whole.

Here's an example. What do you see in the picture in Figure 9?

WHAT DO YOU SEE?

Most likely your answer is "a face," And that answer is correct. Partially. So, look again. What else can you see?

If you are *still* only seeing the face, try tilting your head about 45 degrees to the right.

If you still can't see anything else, you may need to see your optometrist!

By now, you will have discovered the word "Liar" in the diagram. So which is the true view of reality—the face or the word? The obvious answer is "both." In many business situations our perception is limited to only certain aspects of the circumstances. We see the face in the circumstances but miss the word. As we have seen, making decisions about how to respond based on a partial perception or a misperception can be harmful.

Perception can be defined as a process by which individuals organize and interpret their sensory impressions in order to give meaning to their environment. . . . Perception gives rise to individual behavioral responses to particular situations.
—*Rahim Poonjani,*
From Perception to Reality

So the more important question is, "*Why* didn't you see the word 'Liar' right away, since it is clearly there?" To answer this, we need to examine in more detail the actual cognitive dynamics involved in perception. Let's use the face/liar diagram as an example.

Your perception about the "reality" of the diagram was in fact based on two cognitive processes, *noticing* and *sense making.*[3] What your mind probably noticed first was the vertical layout of the box (observe how different the image looks when the box is placed horizontally, as in Figure 10).

Figure 10

NOW WHAT DO YOU SEE?

Based on what you noticed, your mind then made sense of the lines within that box by interpreting them as a face. These two processes—noticing and sense making—happened unconsciously, almost simultaneously (clearly, however, noticing is primary; you can't make sense of something you haven't noticed). These two cognitive processes are always at work in our perception. We notice certain things and not others. Then we make sense of those details.

Leaders need to be highly aware that their perception of reality is inevitably partial and somewhat skewed, and factor that awareness into their decision making and discussions with others.

For instance, in a disagreement with someone, your recounting of the facts is almost certainly going to be a *partial* description, based on your "perception" of the event. You will have noticed certain aspects of the situation, while other details will have escaped your attention altogether. Then, based on your unique experience and current context, your mind will have made sense of those things you noticed.

Of course, the other person is going to describe a *different* perception of the situation, based on a *different* unique mix of noticing and sense making. Differences of opinion as to "what's really going on" may be based on differences of perception. If these differences are significant enough, you may feel that the other person is describing an altogether different reality!

> *The range of what we think and do is limited by what*
> *we fail to notice. And because we fail to notice that we*
> *fail to notice, there is little we can do to change; until*
> *we notice how failing to notice shapes our thoughts*
> *and deeds.*
>
> —*R. D. Laing, psychiatrist*

It's as if we all wear different "perceiving" glasses. The lenses of these glasses determine what we notice and the sense we make of it. Each of us has our own particular "lens prescription," emerging from our unique combination of personality type, life experiences, organizational roles and responsibilities, gender, culture, beliefs, values, and past successes and failures. These elements combine to create a particular set of glasses that we wear to notice and make sense of our world. *Unfortunately, most people are quite unaware that they wear "perceptual glasses."* So accustomed are we to seeing through them, we come to believe that we have no glasses at all. We assume we are seeing reality as it is. When others see something different, we assume they are stupid, weird, wrong, or difficult.

The assumption that we are seeing reality as it actually is, is faulty, and as we saw earlier in this chapter, it can be costly for our leadership effectiveness. Misperceptions can cause leaders to respond to situations with the wrong Leadership Dimensions or the wrong mix of Building Blocks of a Dimension. For example, when you perceive the facts of a situation to be "business as usual" you may be missing or misinterpreting events that actually indicate that you are on the precipice of a crisis.

Clearly, the Leadership Dimensions you would choose to employ would be quite different based on the latter perception. Leaders at IBM were not *stupid* when they failed to perceive the need to focus on micro- and personal computers, not just mainframes. They simply had fallen prey to the very human tendency to misperceive information based on their past successes, current beliefs, and unexamined assumptions. This situation isn't unique. It's routine. And it needs to be confronted for a leader to be successful.

WHAT TINTS YOUR GLASSES?
Two Sources of Misperception

We don't see things as they are, we see things as we are.

—Anaïs Nin, author

There are two specific sources of misperception of which leaders should be aware—"Filter Oblivion," and "No Data/Bad Data." Recognizing these sources will enable you to take strategic action to counteract their effects.

Filter Oblivion

The first source of misperception leaders need to guard against is Filter Oblivion.

Here's an exercise that illustrates this concept. Notice the two stars in Figure 11. Now cover your right eye and, while focusing on the white star on the right, move *very slowly* toward the book. If you move slowly enough, at some point the black star on the left will momentarily disappear.

Figure 11

That is a powerful illustration of the fact that we all have physical blind spots in our perception. There are some points in our vision where we simply cannot see what is actually there. If you needed to be able to see the black star at that point, you would be in trouble.

The same is true mentally. Our perceptual filters cause blind spots when we take in information. If the critical information you need is in one of your mental blind spots, you may make a decision that makes things worse, not better.

Perceptual filters are the mental processes that amplify some stimuli and diminish others. Through this filtering process, information that is determined to be relevant comes into our perceptual foreground, while that which is deemed irrelevant recedes into the background. To put it more simply, our filters determine what we notice.[4]

While perceptual filtering makes the information we notice less complete, it also renders it more understandable. Such filtering is both necessary and useful. For example, a basketball player's ability to obliterate the noise and movement of the crowd while taking a foul shot is a positive use of filtering. Your ability to pay attention to what a client is telling you on your cell phone while walking down a loud street is another. So too is being able to sift through the myriad details of a report to find the information most relevant to a business decision. The ability to filter information is necessary to manage the flood of stimuli that would otherwise overwhelm us. Filtering allows us to attend to the things that are important and ignore the rest.

But perceptual filtering has a downside as well. Sometimes, the information that a person's filters move to the background is actually important. Our filters can create blind spots that can cause us to miss key data and lead to faulty decisions.

Many leaders assume they are seeing reality as it is. They are oblivious to the existence of perceptual filters that operate continuously outside their consciousness. Such Filter Oblivion keeps them from assessing whether there is crucial information they are not seeing, or whether they are misinterpreting those things they do see. Filter Oblivion can thus lead to a poor choice regarding the most appropriate Leadership Dimensions with which to respond to a particular situation.

> *Every person has built up in his or her mind certain usually subconscious assumptions, expectations, and hypotheses about the world in which he or she lives, which profoundly influence how the person perceives events.*
>
> —*Rahim Poonjani,*
> Perception in Organizations

For example, a manager may have a perceptual filter that tends to minimize the relevance of information from frontline staff. On the basis of his or her assumptions, experience, and organizational position, this person may believe (perhaps unconsciously) that workers do not have sufficient perspective to make their suggestions worthwhile. So when a frontline staff member offers a perception about the underlying causes of a problem, the manager may filter out and automatically relegate their comments to the "irrelevant pile." The staff member's information has now been moved into one of the manager's mental blind spots, and the manager's decision will be lacking important information. This process probably happens unconsciously, perhaps even while that manager is promoting the importance of employee contributions!

Sometimes our filters don't just *ignore* information but actually *alter* it! Joel Barker's video *The Business of Paradigms* provides a powerful example of this phenomenon.[5] Barker shows you a series of playing cards at very high speed and asks you to identify them. This series is then replayed several times, with the sequence being slowed down significantly each time. It is only on the slowest replay that most people realize they are looking at several cards that are in the opposite color to what they are supposed to be. In the first several run-throughs, your mind just changes the color of the card to fit with your paradigm about playing cards. Only after several exposures, at increasingly slower speeds, are you able to see what's actually there! It's a startling example of the power of perceptual filters to actually alter what we are looking at and change it to align with our assumptions and beliefs.

> We see what we expect or want to see. All perception occurs in a rich, dynamic, ongoing context, and a thorough understanding of the perceptual process demands that we understand the roles of expectations, assumptions, and hypotheses, which, taken together, constitute what may be called a person's assumptive world.
> —Rahim Poonjani,
> Perception in Organizations

How might this apply to leaders? An area where we have frequently noticed the impact of Filter Oblivion is evaluating a direct report's performance. For example, Anne, a nursing supervisor with whom we recently worked, was lamenting the negative attitude of Theresa, one of her staff members. She cited several examples of Theresa's "selfishness, laziness, and disrespect for her authority." Interestingly, in observing and speaking with Theresa, we noted a deep commitment to the team, a willingness to go the extra mile, and a seemingly genuine desire to work well with Anne. What was going on?

Anne's best friend at work, Barb, had been Theresa's previous supervisor and there had been numerous problems in their working relationship. A combination of inexperience on Barb's part (she was newly promoted to a management role and initially tended to be very controlling), jealousy from Theresa (who didn't get the promotion), and some genuine personality clashing accounted for their relational difficulties. Over time, this had led to an antagonistic relationship between the two.

During this time, Barb had confided in Anne and, consequently, Anne had developed an extremely negative perception of Theresa. When Theresa was transferred to Anne's team, these negative filters influenced what Anne saw in Theresa. Ironically, Theresa told us that she felt this transfer had given her a whole new lease on life, and she was participating in her new team enthusiastically.

Unfortunately, unbeknownst to Theresa, her suggestions to Anne regarding how the team could improve its performance were interpreted as insubordination. Her staying late was interpreted, not as going the extra mile, but as "she must not be getting her work done on time." Her efforts to assist other staff were seen as meddling. Anne's filters actually kept her from seeing Theresa's positive contributions. Such is the power—and potential danger—of perceptual filters.

Filter Oblivion is a natural state. Filters and the blind spots and distortions they create are usually unconscious. It is crucial for you to accept that you *do have* perceptual filters, since acknowledging this will ensure you reassess your conclusions, accounting for possible blind spots and distortions.

Bad Data/No Data

The second source of misperception of which leaders need to be aware is a phenomenon we call Bad Data/No Data. Whereas everyone experiences Filter Oblivion, Bad Data/No Data is a phenomenon specific to leadership positions, and the higher your position, the worse it tends to be!

"Bad Data/No Data" is our phrase to describe the very common (and very understandable) practice of subordinates distorting (Bad Data) or omitting (No Data) information when speaking to their superiors. There are three common causes of this syndrome.

1. **The desire to please the boss.** Sometimes people distort or suppress the facts of a situation in order to avoid their leader's displeasure. Too many leaders tend to "shoot the messenger" rather than thank a subordinate who chooses to be candid about unpleasant information. The stronger the negative reaction from a leader tends to be, the greater the likelihood that subordinates will in future distort or omit information they judge likely to provoke that response.

2. **The desire to be identified as a team player.** Most people have a natural desire to be seen as a team player, or someone who supports the party line. In many settings, a person who brings troubling news to a group's attention receives messages (verbal or otherwise) that such news is unwelcome. Such negative messaging increases the likelihood that information shared with the team will be distorted to fit the "acceptable version of reality."

3. **The desire to be seen as positive.** The individual's normal desire is to be viewed as positive and upbeat, not the organizational crank. If this is reinforced by a leader's attitude that people who discuss unpleasant information are "negativists," it is even more likely that information will be laundered.

Bad Data/No Data is most extreme at the highest levels of leadership. In 1991 John Byrne coined the phrase "CEO Disease" to refer to this phenomenon.[6] The desire to please the boss and avoid possible recrimination for sharing bad news is part of the natural power imbalance between leaders and subordinates. Thus CEOs, who wield the most power in an organization, experience this phenomenon most acutely. Recently, John Sherlock, assistant professor of human resources at Western Carolina University, surveyed several CEOs concerning their challenges in regard to ongoing learning in their role. One of the themes that

Sherlock highlights is the frustration expressed by CEOs about their difficulties in getting the "straight goods" about what is going on. One CEO's comments typify this frustration: "They tell me what I want to hear, and then they sit back in the halls and huddle about what they really believe. It drives me crazy, and I say to them all the time, don't do that. But it doesn't work."[7]

While the problem of Bad Data/No Data is greatest at the most senior levels of an organization, it is a dynamic that anyone with formal leadership authority in a company will have to deal with. In situations where information is being filtered up from the bottom of an organization to higher levels, the information is likely to be altered somewhat at each layer. By the time it reaches senior levels, the story may tell a rather different tale from what is actually occurring at the grassroots level.

To be clear, we are not suggesting that individuals are intentionally trying to undermine an organization or that they are unethical and untrustworthy. The three causes of Bad Data/No Data are very powerful psychological forces, often acting in concert with one another. These forces are difficult to resist—even for senior leaders.

The executive team of one of our clients recently experienced the power of these forces. A regional director had not disclosed to the CEO that a high level of frustration and resentment existed in the region, caused by a number of recent major changes in organizational procedures. When the CEO dropped in for a visit while in the region, she was inundated with complaints and accusations from managers and staff alike. The CEO was caught off guard and felt ill equipped to respond. Needless to say, she wasn't pleased. Later, she learned that her direct report had not intentionally tried to deceive her. He had simply fallen prey to the natural desire to be seen in the best light possible and to avoid the CEO's wrath (something she had been prone to express in the past but is now trying to control).

Individuals do not usually have malicious motives in "adjusting" the facts they are communicating. They may not even be aware that they are suppressing or distorting information. The power dynamics between leaders and their followers naturally create conditions in which Bad Data/No Data will flourish unless consciously countered.

In situations where a leader's knowledge of the circumstances is significantly based on information from subordinates, the leader needs to ascertain to what extent the Bad Data/No Data phenomenon is at play before deciding which Leadership Dimensions to use.

We have now seen two common and powerful sources of misperception: Filter Oblivion and Bad Data/No Data. These two phenomena are often *both* present, furthering the possibility that a leader's perception of reality is not fully accurate. What, then, can a leader do to combat their effects?

CLEARING UP YOUR VISION
Strategies and Tactics to Better See Reality

To see what is in front of one's nose needs a constant struggle.

—George Orwell, author

Misperception may be common, but it is not insurmountable. While total perception of reality may be beyond human capacity, *sufficient* perception is not. There are a number of strategies and tactics leaders can employ to overcome the detrimental effects of both Filter Oblivion and Bad Data/No Data. What follows are seven of the most important strategies and tactics to help you better see your reality.

1. **Genuinely accept that you fail to fully see reality.** By now you should be convinced that misperception happens frequently. The next step is to admit that it happens frequently to *you!* Everyone has filters, and most leaders experience some degree of Bad Data/ No Data when dealing with their subordinates. Unless you genuinely accept that your perceptions are often skewed or partial you are unlikely to take the remaining suggestions seriously. So the question is "Do you truly believe that you—at least sometimes— misperceive reality?"

   Accepting this truth means that, whenever possible, you need to withhold judgment until you have explored the situation from multiple perspectives. While there are some situations—primarily crises—that demand an immediate decision, in most cases, leaders can afford to question their assumptions and perspectives and seek a fuller understanding of the situation.

2. **Cultivate a climate of mutual trust and openness.** The more leaders are able to create trust-based relationships with their direct reports, the less those individuals will feel the need to avoid speaking unpleasant truths. The more individuals feel their opinions, concerns, and perspectives are genuinely desired and appreciated, the more likely they will be to voice them. Trust and openness are central to combating misperception.

3. **Give up the search for someone to blame when things don't go right.** In an article titled "Jim Collins Speaks the Truth," Collins states, "One of the constant, pervasive, and dampening effects on being able to confront the brutal facts is the search for people to blame for things that went wrong or didn't work. Instead of blaming people, leaders need to look at this work as an autopsy, an attempt to try and understand what actually happened and not to assign blame to individuals."[8]

Disciplining themselves to refrain from assigning blame can be tough for leaders, but it is necessary to sustain a climate in which the truth may be freely pursued.

4. **Face the fear of knowing the truth.** Sometimes the implications of reality are so unpleasant that leaders choose to ignore what is actually occurring. While offering short-term relief, this "head in the sand" approach is usually a recipe for disaster. In explaining the contrasting recent histories of the grocery store chains Kroeger and A&P, Jim Collins argues that A&P's decline was rooted in their unwillingness in the early 1970s to face the financial and human investments demanded by the emerging trend toward superstores. They ignored the real problem (the need to completely renovate their stores) and focused instead on changing CEOs and trying to cut costs. In contrast, Kroeger faced the facts, felt the fear, and decided to get on with revamping their stores, one by one. Collins concludes by stating, "I observe that it is not the brutal facts themselves that people have difficulty confronting but their inevitable consequences."[9]

Facing the fear of knowing the truth does take courage, but it is fundamental to overcoming both Filter Oblivion and Bad Data/ No Data. Failure to admit our fears ensures that they will act as a filter. Acknowledging them reduces their filtering potential. Openly confronting others' fears and concerns will help them overcome their natural reluctance to see what is actually occurring, enabling them to provide data that is more reality based.

5. **Look for the exceptional.** This strategy, suggested by Starbuck and Milliken, is particularly relevant to Filter Oblivion.[10] Since our filters cause us to see what we expect to see, we need to look intentionally for the things that don't make sense within our current frameworks. This involves seeking out data, trends, or actions that don't fit our expectations. These observations may be disorienting and revealing and can be an important corrective to our biases, assumptions, and beliefs.

You will recall the story of the medical supervisor whose perception of her staff member was heavily influenced by her friendship with that staff member's previous supervisor. Had this supervisor intentionally looked for behaviors that deviated from her expectations, she may have come to realize that her perception of this staff member was more *illusion* than *reality*. This would have permitted her to choose a more appropriate leadership response in working with her.

6. **Create structures and systems that build in multiple perspectives.** While differences of perspective sometimes lead to tension and arguments, they are also crucial in overcoming individual and group perceptual filters. The more we create structures and processes that elicit different perspectives, the more likely it is that our filters will be exposed, allowing us to develop a fuller picture of our circumstances. Having these structures sends the message that no one person's perspective fully expresses the truth. Having formal processes in place assures that all relevant voices are heard, not just those that are more assertive or more likeable.

Such structures include regular face-to-face team discussions, one-on-one consultations with relevant parties, email discussion lists, and video/telephone conferencing. It is important that the structures be used regularly and that all participants' input be respected and considered.

7. **Seek outside data.** At times, the power of individual and group filters is so strong, we need someone from the outside to help us see more clearly what is really going on. While there is a risk that an outsider may misunderstand or underappreciate certain events or information, the greater likelihood is that the fresh perspective will help us see information we have ignored or undervalued. Outside data can be obtained in numerous ways. Associating with industry peers in either formal or informal networks (in person or online) is one means. Reading journals and newspapers is another. Bringing in consultants or coaches, attending conferences, and simply talking with peers in a different department can all be means by which we free ourselves of Filter Oblivion by seeking outside data.

CONCLUSION

Implementing these seven suggestions will enable you to manage misperceptions and gain a greater grasp of reality. Seeing reality more clearly will then enable you to choose the Leadership Dimensions most appropriate for your context.

CHAPTER 8

HOW DO YOU GAIN 20/20 VISION?

SEEING YOUR CONTEXT CLEARLY

The real act of discovery consists not in finding new lands but in seeing with new eyes.

—Marcel Proust

Lasting leadership effectiveness is achieved by continually adapting your leadership approach to the current context. The ability to see your context clearly is obviously a prerequisite for choosing the most appropriate Leadership Dimensions in response. Now that you have several strategies to enable you to perceive reality more fully, we are going to explore seven common contexts leaders encounter and the Leadership Dimensions that are most appropriate to them. By providing a template that you can apply to your context, these patterns should help you determine which Leadership Dimensions will create maximum effectiveness in your setting.

Of course, to some degree every organization's context is unique. Numerous factors combine to create this distinctiveness:

- The industry in which the company works and that industry's current status in the larger economy

- The history of the company and its consequent reputation

- The status of its competitors

- The technological infrastructure of the company

- The composition of the organization's leadership team

- The composition of the company's workforce

- The organization's culture

The list could be extended, but the point is that no two organizations are identical. Each organization's context—its environment, its culture, its total identity—is unique.

At the same time, the seven business contexts discussed in this chapter cross the boundaries of industry, company history, technology, and individual personalities. So while you certainly need to consider the implications of unique or exceptional factors in your setting, you will probably find that one or more of these contextual patterns fits sufficiently well that the recommendations offered in this chapter can be directly applied to your own organization.

BUSINESS CONTEXT #1
Rapid Growth

All the challenges and obstacles of leading . . . are magnified when the firm is growing rapidly. There is heightened pressure to constantly change and innovate in every aspect of managing.

—The Growth Builders Report

So, business is booming! That's great news, but it does bring its own challenges for leaders—challenges that, if not handled well, could lead not only to stagnation but to future decline.

Rapid growth is a contextual pattern characterized by a marked increase in the number of sales, the volume of business, the financial costs, and the demand on employees. Occasionally, it is unexpected—consumer demand for your product or service seems to come out of nowhere, catching the business off guard, sending everyone into a frenzy of activity just trying to keep up. More often, rapid growth is intentional —the result of a conscious commitment, solid planning, and aggressive action by the senior leadership of the group. Rapid growth may be experienced by the entire company or may be confined to certain departments or business units.

Periods of rapid growth require both wise management and strong leadership (for the distinctions between these two aspects of a manager's role, see Appendix B). The management challenges during times of rapid growth include

- Scheduling and/or hiring staff to adequately meet demand

- Coordinating between departments to maximize efficiencies

- Allocating financial resources to key areas

- Planning to increase capacity if ongoing rapid growth is desired

Depending on your level of leadership in the organization, you may or may not be involved directly in these management tasks. Regardless of your position, the Leadership Dimensions most applicable to times of rapid growth are the same.

Before you learn about *our* perspective on which of the five Dimensions are most relevant to leading in a time of rapid growth, take a few moments to record *your* ideas in Tool 10. Doing so will allow you to assess how much you have already internalized about the Dimensions and how they apply.

Tool 10

LEADERSHIP DIMENSIONS FOR RAPID GROWTH

Directions: In the column on the left, list the Leadership Dimensions you think are most appropriate for leading in a rapid growth context. On the right, explain your rationale for choosing that Dimension.

Leadership Dimension   **Rationale**

- _____   - _____

                                _____

- _____   - _____

                                _____

- _____   - _____

                                _____

- _____   - _____

                                _____

Now, in the left-hand column below, rank the Dimensions you listed above in order of priority (importance to desired outcome) and/or sequence (the order in which you would apply them).

Leadership Dimension   **Your Reasoning for This Order**
Ranking   **(priority and/or sequence)**

1. _____

2. _____

3. _____

4. _____

Here is *our* ranking of the Leadership Dimensions most effective in a context of rapid growth, with a rationale to follow:

1. Visioning

2. Enrolling

3. Coaching

Visioning

For two reasons, Visioning is the primary Leadership Dimension needed during times of rapid growth. First, when the vision is clear and compelling, people need far fewer specific directions, freeing the leader to focus on the broader issues related to sustaining growth. Staff can make many decisions themselves when they know the overall direction and believe it to be worthwhile. Second, times of rapid growth usually require staff members to work hard for long hours. Vision supplies the motivation to persevere when things are intensely busy for long periods of time. When people can connect their effort to a worthwhile vision, they are better able to sustain their energy. For these reasons, keeping people focused on the vision is critical. As one CEO puts it, "The plan doesn't make you successful; communicating the company's thinking and vision does."[1]

> *It is very common for a [leader] to think his vision is clear to everyone because he thinks of little else and it's extremely clear to him. But often, the thinking behind the vision hasn't been shared, so people have a sort of one-dimensional view of the vision that doesn't help them in translating it into methodologies, systems, and plans that work.*
> —*Katherine Catlin, author*

Enrolling

The second Dimension needed for times of rapid growth is Enrolling. It might be assumed that the strong pressure on people's time during rapid growth would preclude the use of this Dimension as it can be time-consuming. Even though there are significant time pressures in the midst of growth, they are usually related to the amount of hours people are required to work, not the speed at which decisions have to be made (unlike in a crisis). Sustaining rapid growth requires time spent strategizing and planning. Bringing forth ideas that will continue to drive growth and developing consensus around implementing these ideas are two key benefits of using the Enrolling Dimension in this context. These benefits make Enrolling worth the time.

Coaching

The third Dimension beneficial for times of rapid growth is Coaching. As a business grows, so too does the need for more leaders. Typically, top performers in the company are promoted into new managerial responsibilities. In many companies, these individuals receive little or no coaching or training for their new responsibilities and lack the skills needed to be successful. Employing Coaching remedies this problem, increasing the likelihood that growth will continue.

These three Dimensions—Visioning, Enrolling, and Coaching—need to be used simultaneously for a business to sustain strong growth.

BUSINESS CONTEXT #2
Fast Paced

For almost any business these days, speed is indeed life.
—Bob Davis, founder of Lycos

The pace of life in most organizations is on average much faster than even ten years ago. Nonetheless, certain businesses and some departments within organizations operate at an even faster pace than average (for example, hospital emergency departments, call centers, advertising agencies, and stock brokerages). What defines the fast-paced business context is that the speed of operations is above average, continual, and a necessity of the business. In the fast-paced company or department people are always in motion, meetings are marked by a sense of urgency, and conversations are frequently quick and intense.

When effective leadership is not present in the fast-paced context, several negative dynamics typically emerge—dynamics that carry significant financial and human costs. The high levels of stress typically experienced by staff in these settings can lead to decreasing productivity, increased mistakes, frayed relationships, and burnout. The speed of operations often leads to miscommunication, resulting in mistakes and time wasted in redoing work. Constant activity can crowd out the time needed for reflection, experimentation, and strategizing—three practices necessary for ongoing innovation. Finally, a fast pace often causes people to lose sight of priorities—the all-too-common confusing of the urgent with the important.

Given the potential costs of the fast-paced context, what Dimensions should a leader employ to counter them? Before we provide our answer to that question, take a few moments to record your ideas in Tool 11.

Tool 11

LEADERSHIP DIMENSIONS FOR FAST PACED

Directions: In the column on the left, list the Leadership Dimensions you think are most appropriate for leading in a fast-paced context. On the right, explain your rationale for choosing that Dimension.

Leadership Dimension   **Rationale**

- _____   - _____
                             _____

- _____   - _____
                             _____

- _____   - _____
                             _____

- _____   - _____
                             _____

Now, in the left-hand column below, rank the Dimensions you listed above in order of priority (importance to desired outcome) and/or sequence (the order in which you would apply them).

Leadership Dimension   **Your Reasoning for This Order**
Ranking   **(priority and/or sequence)**

1. _____

2. _____

3. _____

4. _____

Here is our ranking of the Leadership Dimensions most effective in a fast-paced context:

1. Visioning

2. Relating

3. Coaching

Visioning

The importance of Visioning in a fast-paced context is twofold: First, in a hectic environment people easily lose sight of priorities and long-term goals, confusing what is important with what feels urgent. Visioning draws people back to priorities and helps them make the best decisions in a pressure-filled setting. Second, Visioning helps recharge people's motivational batteries. It is easy to "grow weary in well-doing" in a fast-paced context. Regularly reminding people of the value of the work they are doing and what the group is trying to achieve together helps sustain enthusiasm and commitment.

Relating

Very close in importance to Visioning is the Relating Dimension. High levels of stress, misunderstandings, and angry outbursts are not uncommon in a fast-paced context. These quickly take their toll on relationships, making the workplace less appealing to those who work there. Applications of Relating that can help alleviate the negative impacts of the pace of work include attending to conflict, trying to inject humor and fun into the mix, and spending time individually with your team members. Taking time with each person on a regular basis allows you to judge how the person is handling the workload and pace, and to be proactive in providing support or time off if the person needs it. Furthermore, investing time with a person in a busy environment communicates implicitly that he or she matters to you—a powerful source of motivation.

Coaching

The third Dimension important when leading in a fast-paced context is Coaching. Even with the best leadership, an environment of constant speed causes significant stress. The coaching that needs to take place in this setting typically concerns issues of stress management, time management, and skill development in workers' tasks (so they can accomplish their work with maximum efficiency and minimum stress). As with Relating, the time spent coaching your staff in the midst of a busy environment communicates implicitly that your staff are important to you. The return in loyalty, commitment, and motivation makes the time investment more than worthwhile.

BUSINESS CONTEXT #3
Sudden Crisis

Next week there can't be any crisis. My schedule is already full.

—Henry Kissinger, former secretary of state

Crises are never convenient. But they are inevitable.

When we speak of a sudden crisis as a business context, we are referring to unanticipated events that demand an immediate response. These include both human tragedies, such as those caused by a hurricane or flood, and business crises like the dot.com bust. While some crises emerge from our own inaction or poor decision making, the crises we have in mind are primarily those that are caused by factors beyond our control.

Such circumstances have three primary characteristics to which leaders must respond. First, people are usually highly anxious and/or afraid. Their worries and fears may center on their personal safety (such as during the SARS crisis in Toronto in 2003) or their economic situation. Second, circumstances demand a rapid response. There is little time for deliberation or research in a sudden crisis—immediate action is called for. Third, quick fixes are the initial priority. To borrow a medical analogy, in a sudden crisis leaders need to stop the "hemorrhaging" before all else.

Given these dynamics, what Dimensions should a leader employ to best respond to a sudden crisis? Before we provide our answer to that question, take a few moments to record your ideas in Tool 12.

Tool 12

LEADERSHIP DIMENSIONS FOR SUDDEN CRISIS

Directions: In the column on the left, list the Leadership Dimensions you think are most appropriate for leading in a context of sudden crisis. On the right, explain your rationale for choosing that Dimension.

Leadership Dimension   **Rationale**

- _____   - _____
                                _____

- _____   - _____
                                _____

- _____   - _____
                                _____

- _____   - _____
                                _____

Now, in the left-hand column below, rank the Dimensions you listed above in order of priority (importance to desired outcome) and/or sequence (the order in which you would apply them).

**Leadership Dimension   Your Reasoning for This Order
Ranking   (priority and/or sequence)**

1. _____

2. _____

3. _____

4. _____

Here is our ranking of the Leadership Dimensions most effective in a sudden crisis context:

1. Commanding

2. Visioning

3. Relating

Commanding

Commanding is the primary Dimension leaders need to employ when facing a sudden crisis. In times of uncertainty and fear, people want a leader who is decisive, confident, and clear about what actions need to be taken. Furthermore, sudden crises require a rapid response. Quick decisions and immediate action are two of the hallmarks of Commanding.

Visioning

The second Dimension that leaders need to employ in a context of sudden crisis is Visioning. After the emotional shock that attends the onset of a crisis, people often feel desolation and despair. Leaders need to provide a sense of hope for the future and inspire people to take immediate action to begin rebuilding. Visioning paints pictures of a desired future and thus inspires action. Constant communication of a message of hope is critical after the initial shock of the sudden crisis wears off.

Relating

The third Dimension that is often useful in a sudden crisis is Relating. Again, after the initial shock of the crisis has passed, people often feel fearful, anxious, and uncertain. Taking even small amounts of time to chat with people to ask how they are doing makes a significant difference. It offers them consolation and encouragement. Furthermore, when people know you care, they are more willing to follow your commands.

If you review our account in Chapter 1 of Giuliani's amazing response to 9/11, you will see all three of these Dimensions embedded in his actions during that fateful time.

Together (and usually introduced in the order in which we have listed them) these three Leadership Dimensions allow leaders to make the best of calamitous circumstances.

BUSINESS CONTEXT #4
Blended Family

*It is the function of creative men to perceive the rela-
tions between [things] that may seem utterly different,
and to be able to combine them into some new forms—
the power to connect the seemingly unconnected.*

—*William Plomer, South African man of letters*

One of the signs of the times in our society is the large number of blended
families that now populate the domestic scene. The challenges of merging two formerly distinct family units are significant.

Similarly, in the past fifteen to twenty years many organizations and
teams have had to learn how to work in blended families. The large
number of mergers and acquisitions (M&As) is one cause of these. The
other is the increased frequency of company reorganizations that move
people from one team or department to another. Let's look briefly at each
of these factors.

M&As

Mergers and acquisitions have been a key strategy for many organizations in their attempts to increase market share and sustain growth. All
too often, the results fall far below expectations. In fact, estimates suggest
that somewhere between two-thirds and three-quarters of M&As fail to
realize their intended financial goals.[2]

The leadership challenges encountered in the context of a merger or
acquisition are significant—and often poorly handled. Here are just
some of these challenges:

- The blending of two distinct corporate cultures

- The anxieties and resentment of staff who fear losing power,
  position, and even employment

- The lack of trust between individuals from the two companies

- The merging of different technologies, policies, and procedures to which people have been accustomed

What should be clear from this list is that the critical factors to which leaders must attend are the people issues. While the importance of the financial and technological aspects should not be undervalued, it is the "softer" people issues that most frequently derail the process and account for the common failures of M&As.

> *It is true that the consideration of the people affected is limited. M&A transactions are normally decided, planned and executed by a small group of executives (who are likely, but not necessarily, to benefit from them). The rest of the organisation is the object, not the subject of the integration process.*
> *—Silvio Conforti, mergers & acquisitions specialist, Union Bank of Switzerland*

Reorganization

The other common cause of the blended-family context is a company or departmental reorganization. In such circumstances, employees may know each other to a limited degree, but typically they have not worked with one another, so issues of trust, anxiety, and resentment are likely to be present. Furthermore, significant differences between the departmental or team cultures to which people have become accustomed are often overlooked by leaders. It is often assumed that since everyone has been working for the same company there shouldn't be many hurdles in moving from one part of the organization to another. In fact, department and team cultures can differ significantly within the same organization. Thus, as with mergers and acquisitions, addressing interpersonal issues in cases of company reorganizations is critical to achieve the productivity that the reorganization is intended to create.

So, how do leaders address the dynamics of a blended-family context? Before we provide our answer to that question, take a few moments to record your ideas in Tool 13.

Tool 13

LEADERSHIP DIMENSIONS FOR BLENDED FAMILY

Directions: In the column on the left, list the Leadership Dimensions you think are most appropriate for leading in a context of blended family. On the right, explain your rationale for choosing that Dimension.

Leadership Dimension   **Rationale**

▪ _____   ▪ _____

                                _____

▪ _____   ▪ _____

                                _____

▪ _____   ▪ _____

                                _____

▪ _____   ▪ _____

                                _____

Now, in the left-hand column below, rank the Dimensions you listed above in order of priority (importance to desired outcome) and/or sequence (the order in which you would apply them).

Leadership Dimension   **Your Reasoning for This Order**
Ranking   **(priority and/or sequence)**

1. _____

2. _____

3. _____

4. _____

Here is our ranking of the Leadership Dimensions most effective in a blended-family context:

1. Visioning

2. Relating

3. Commanding

Visioning and Relating

Visioning and Relating are equally important in a blended-family context. Visioning helps create a sense of togetherness about a worthwhile future, particularly if the process of creating the vision for the new group is a participative one. Such a process begins to build a sense of enthusiasm, countering some of the anxiety and apprehension that is likely present in most individuals. Talking together about what can be achieved collectively begins to build bridges of communication, create trust, and develop an appreciation for differing strengths. Leaders need to make sure that the vision that emerges for the newly blended group is truly a joint vision, not the imposition of the dominant group's goals over the other's.

Visioning needs to be accompanied by Relating in leading a blended family. The well-known stages of group dynamics in any new team—forming, storming, norming, and performing—are sure to be active. But the challenges of navigating through the first three of these stages are heightened by the dynamics engendered by M&As and reorganizations. Thus, leaders need to attend very carefully to issues like these:

- Cultivating open communication

- Resolving conflicts

- Building trust

- Establishing new norms and procedures that take everyone's concerns into account

- Merging the best aspects of the organizational or departmental cultures from which individual team members come

Commanding

The third Leadership Dimension that may be required in a blended-family context is Commanding. Two particular circumstances may exist for which Commanding is the appropriate Dimension. The first of these concerns staff who will be rendered redundant by the M&A or reorganization. False promises stating that none of them are going to lose their jobs should be avoided, as this only leads to cynicism and lack of trust later. Decisions regarding who is being let go need to be made quickly. The unpleasant news regarding these terminations should be announced clearly and as soon as possible. This decisiveness is necessary to preempt rumors, negativity, and the anxiety that uncertainty creates.

The other circumstance in which Commanding may be necessary occurs when a staff member demonstrates an ongoing unwillingness or inability to "blend" with the family. In these cases, when Visioning and Relating have proved insufficient to gain the person's cooperation and commitment, a stronger approach is necessary. The individual's negative attitudes and behaviors will need to be confronted directly and compliance mandated. In some cases, termination will need to be the ultimate outcome.

BUSINESS CONTEXT #5
Expert Concentration

An expert is someone who knows some of the worst mistakes which can be made, in a very narrow field.

—Neils Bohr, Danish physicist

A short time ago, we had the opportunity to work with the executive team of a genetic research company. It was fascinating to spend several hours with people who were talking in English but speaking a whole other language! During the discussion we discovered that of a company with 125 employees, more than half were scientists. That's a scientific example of what we mean by the expert-concentration context. Expert concentration occurs in companies or departments that comprise mostly highly specialized workers—a phenomenon increasingly common in our knowledge-based, technology-driven economy.

While the knowledge that experts bring to their organizations is invaluable, the dynamics created by a company or department heavily populated with experts can pose significant leadership challenges. These are the three most common:

- A tendency to value research and technology at the expense of profits

- A potential deficit of social skills that negatively impacts team work and customer relations[3]

- A smaller-than-average pool of people who possess the relational skills necessary to be successfully promoted into management and leadership positions

So, which Leadership Dimensions are most relevant in an expert-concentration context? Before we give our answer to that question, take a few moments to record your ideas in Tool 14.

Tool 14

LEADERSHIP DIMENSIONS FOR EXPERT CONCENTRATION

Directions: In the column on the left, list the Leadership Dimensions you think are most appropriate for leading in a context of expert concentration. On the right, explain your rationale for choosing that Dimension.

Leadership Dimension   **Rationale**

- _____   - _____
                                _____

- _____   - _____
                                _____

- _____   - _____
                                _____

- _____   - _____
                                _____

Now, in the left-hand column below, rank the Dimensions you listed above in order of priority (importance to desired outcome) and/or sequence (the order in which you would apply them).

Leadership Dimension Ranking   **Your Reasoning for This Order (priority and/or sequence)**

1. _____

2. _____

3. _____

4. _____

Here is our ranking of the Leadership Dimensions most effective in an expert-concentration context:

1. Coaching

2. Relating

3. Visioning

Coaching

The Leadership Dimension most useful in an expert-concentration context is Coaching. Coaching deals directly with all three of our ranked challenges. (1) Discussing the relationship between a staff member's work and company profitability so as to focus attention on organizational priorities is essentially a coaching conversation. (2) Coaching allows a leader to help a staff member develop greater social awareness and skill in relating more effectively with other staff members or customers. (3) Coaching is the primary means any company needs to employ to expand its leadership base.

> *It is, after all, the responsibility of the expert to operate the familiar and that of the leader to transcend it.*
> —Henry Kissinger,
> former secretary of state

Coaching is critical for leading in an expert concentration.

Relating

The Relating Dimension is often needed as well, particularly when experts work in a team environment with less technically specialized individuals (either from the same department or across departments). The Relating Dimension addresses the problems that emerge most commonly in these mixed teams: communication challenges, differing values, and conflict. Improving mutual understanding, building a sense of unity, and mediating conflict are all applications of Relating that are often needed in such a mixed team.

Visioning

Finally, leaders will need to use the Visioning Dimension on a regular basis in an expert-concentration context. The focus on research or technical knowledge often becomes an end in itself for experts. Consequently there is often a need to refocus people on the bigger picture—what the team, department, or organization is ultimately trying to accomplish. This allows people to better prioritize their time when working on research projects.

BUSINESS CONTEXT #6
Civil War

A house divided against itself cannot stand.

—Abraham Lincoln, former president

There is a good reason the Civil War still looms large in the American psyche, although it occurred almost 150 years ago. A civil war wrenches the soul of a nation, inflicting psychological wounds from which it take ages to recover. On a smaller scale, "civil wars" in the workplace wrench the soul of a business, leaving emotional and financial scars that do not heal quickly.[4]

A business context of civil war is one in which conflict is

- Overt: the parties in the conflict make no attempt to hide their disdain and disagreements from each other

- Pervasive: rather than the dispute involving just a few, the majority of the group has aligned with one side or the other; few are able or willing to remain neutral

- Protracted: the conflict is long lasting

Civil war can happen in a team, within a department, between departments, between regions, or between management and labor. Organizational civil wars are immensely destructive, ravaging relationships, destroying trust and goodwill, and breeding resentment and grudges that can last for years.

Just as preventive medicine is preferable to crisis intervention, so, too, dealing well with conflict in its early stages is obviously greatly preferable to trying to halt a civil war. When leaders are leading well, using the appropriate Dimensions to address circumstances as they emerge, civil war can usually be avoided. However, if you are in the midst of a civil war (whether it emerged under your watch or whether you inherited it), it is critical to know how to address this painful situation.

So, what Dimensions do leaders have to employ to deal with this destructive context? Before we provide our answer to that question, take a few moments to record your ideas in Tool 15.

Tool 15

LEADERSHIP DIMENSIONS FOR CIVIL WAR

Directions: In the column on the left, list the Leadership Dimensions you think are most appropriate for leading in a context of civil war. On the right, explain your rationale for choosing that Dimension.

Leadership Dimension   **Rationale**

- _____   - _____
                                _____

- _____   - _____
                                _____

- _____   - _____
                                _____

- _____   - _____
                                _____

Now, in the left-hand column below, rank the Dimensions you listed above in order of priority (importance to desired outcome) and/or sequence (the order in which you would apply them).

**Leadership Dimension
Ranking**

**Your Reasoning for This Order
(priority and/or sequence)**

1. _____

2. _____

3. _____

4. _____

Here is our ranking of the Leadership Dimensions most effective in a civil war context:

1. Relating

2. Visioning

3. Commanding

Relating

Relating is the primary Dimension to use because mediation will be needed (assuming the factions are willing to explore the causes of the conflict and look for mutually agreeable solutions). Even if mediation is successful, lingering suspicion, resentment, and hurt feelings will require a leader to continue to work on restoring trust and goodwill. Vigilance must be exercised in clarifying communication, nipping little irritants in the bud, and dealing with rumors and innuendo. It takes a long time for people to begin to trust one another after protracted periods of intense conflict.

> *You can't shake hands with a clenched fist.*
> —Indira Gandhi, former prime minister of India

Visioning

Dealing with the roots of conflict through the Relating Dimension is the necessary first step. The next step, appealing to a vision that all parties find worthwhile, can encourage them to take mediation seriously and implement agreements reached. Thus, Visioning is also an important Dimension in overcoming civil war. Through Visioning we attempt to lift people's eyes above their grievances and hurt feelings to gaze at a positive future that can be realized together. Through Visioning we appeal to people's better selves.

Commanding

Unfortunately, not all people are willing to let go of the past and try to repair broken relationships. In some cases, individuals will try to sabotage any efforts to create peace or will refuse to act on agreements that have been reached. Appealing to the values of harmony, openness, and goodwill sometimes falls on deaf ears. In these cases, Commanding will be needed either to (1) mandate compliance or (2) remove individuals who are unwilling or unable to let go of the past.

BUSINESS CONTEXT #7
Smooth Sailing

If it ain't broke, don't fix it.
—Anonymous

If it ain't broke, break it.
—Anonymous

There are times in a business when everything is just fine. The volume of business is good and growing, but not at the frantic pace characteristic of the rapid-growth context. Things get hectic at times, but generally things are far from the relentless frenzy of the fast-paced context. No crises are looming on the horizon. And while staff members might squabble occasionally, generally everyone is working well together. Even the experts and generalists seem to be speaking the same language. Profits are good. Shareholders are happy. In short, life is good!

While your business may never be quite this idyllic, there are often protracted periods of time when the context is essentially one of smooth sailing. These times are certainly less frequent than thirty or forty years ago, given the turbulence of our era, but many organizations do experience significant periods of relative stability.

The great danger, of course, is to be lulled into a sense of false security. In our age, where both opportunities and calamities can emerge with lightning speed, leaders must always exercise vigilance. More important, however, times of relative stability provide an organization, department, or team with opportunities to strengthen itself through

- Capacity building: increasing the level and breadth of staff members' skills

- Leadership development: identifying and developing people who show potential for future formal leadership positions

- Innovation: introducing new or improved processes, services, and technology that improve quality, speed, or enjoyment

Leaders will find that the appropriate response in a context of smooth sailing is "If it ain't broke, strengthen it."

So, in a context of smooth sailing, which Dimensions are most important? Before we provide our answer to that question, take a few moments to record your ideas in Tool 16.

Tool 16

LEADERSHIP DIMENSIONS FOR SMOOTH SAILING

Directions: In the column on the left, list the Leadership Dimensions you think are most appropriate for leading in a context of smooth sailing. On the right, explain your rationale for choosing that Dimension.

Leadership Dimension   **Rationale**

- _____   - _____

                               _____

- _____   - _____

                               _____

- _____   - _____

                               _____

- _____   - _____

                               _____

Now, in the left-hand column below, rank the Dimensions you listed above in order of priority (importance to desired outcome) and/or sequence (the order in which you would apply them).

Leadership Dimension   **Your Reasoning for This Order**
Ranking   **(priority and/or sequence)**

1. _____

2. _____

3. _____

4. _____

Here is our ranking of the Leadership Dimensions most effective in a smooth-sailing context:

1. Coaching

2. Visioning

3. Enrolling

4. Relating

Coaching

Coaching is the most obvious way of strengthening individuals and teams. It is the most effective way to enable people to improve current skills or learn new ones. It is by far the best means of developing future leaders.

Visioning and Enrolling

Both Visioning and Enrolling are useful for maintaining people's motivation and for encouraging innovation. Visioning reminds people of the value of what the group is trying to achieve and motivates excellence by providing meaning to what people do on a daily basis. Enrolling keeps people involved through participating in innovation.

Relating

Finally, Relating maintains strong channels of free-flowing communication in an organization. This fosters the sharing of innovative practices and technologies. It also enhances the likelihood of leaders picking up quickly on any information that suggests the company may be leaving smooth waters for a different context. When relationships are strong, communication flows freely.

SUMMARIZING YOUR DISCOVERIES
Determining Your Context

Common sense is the knack of seeing things as they are,
and doing things as they ought to be done.

—Josh Billings (1818–1885) U.S. writer

Tool 17 offers the opportunity to identify which of the seven contexts profiled here fits your current circumstances. In fact, you may find that two, three, or even four of these contexts apply at the same time.

CONCLUSION

Context is dynamic, not static. Your leadership context is ever shifting. This chapter has given you the opportunity to take a snapshot of your current context, to see your present reality more clearly. But your context is sure to evolve. External factors, organizational dynamics, and the *results of your leadership* will cause your contexts to shift. So the process you have been through in these pages is one that you will be undertaking continually. You may not always choose to evaluate your contexts as methodically as you have just done, but you must be constantly assessing what is happening—striving to see your context clearly. Only then can you apply the Leadership Dimensions that will gain you the greatest possible leverage to move your world.

Tool 17

MY CONTEXTS AT A GLANCE

Context #1 **Rapid Growth**	Context #2 **Fast Paced**	Context #3 **Sudden Crisis**
Characteristics That Fit ☐ Marked increase in sales ☐ Marked increase in volume of business ☐ Marked increase in costs ☐ Marked increase in demands on staff **Leadership Dimensions to Use** ☐ Visioning ☐ Enrolling ☐ Coaching	**Characteristics That Fit** ☐ High speed is continual and necessary ☐ People are always in motion ☐ Meetings are marked by urgency ☐ Conversations are quick and intense **Leadership Dimensions to Use** ☐ Visioning ☐ Relating ☐ Coaching	**Characteristics That Fit** ☐ A tragedy or business crisis exists ☐ Staff are anxious, fearful ☐ An immediate response is required **Leadership Dimensions to Use** ☐ Commanding ☐ Visioning ☐ Relating
Context #4 **Blended Family**	Context #5 **Expert Concentration**	Context #6 **Civil War**
Characteristics That Fit ☐ Two or more groups have recently merged ☐ Distinct cultures existed in the groups ☐ Different policies, procedures, and technology existed in the groups ☐ Mistrust or resentment exists in the new group **Leadership Dimensions to Use** ☐ Visioning ☐ Relating ☐ Commanding	**Characteristics That Fit** ☐ Large number of specialists in the group ☐ Tendency to focus on research over profits ☐ Deficit of social skills in many experts **Leadership Dimensions to Use** ☐ Coaching ☐ Relating ☐ Visioning	**Characteristics That Fit** ☐ Existence of overt major conflict ☐ Existence of pervasive major conflict ☐ Existence of protracted major conflict ☐ Existence of clearly defined "camps" **Leadership Dimensions to Use** ☐ Relating ☐ Visioning ☐ Commanding
	Context #7 **Smooth Sailing**	
	Characteristics That Fit ☐ Steady but not overwhelming growth ☐ Steady pace with occasional bursts of speed ☐ Good relationships between staff ☐ Stakeholders are generally satisfied **Leadership Dimensions to Use** ☐ Coaching ☐ Visioning ☐ Enrolling ☐ Relating	

PART 4

LEVERAGING YOUR LEADERSHIP STRENGTHS

Lasting leadership effectiveness requires the ability to shift among Leadership Dimensions in order to match the demands of the immediate business context. In the final section of the book we will help you consolidate the insights you have gained and determine how to act on them to increase your personal leadership effectiveness.

Chapter 9 begins by helping you determine the size of the gap that exists between the Leadership Dimensions your current context requires and the strengths you already possess. The latter half of the chapter provides strategies for enhancing your effectiveness when there is a small gap between what is needed and what you naturally possess.

Chapter 10 provides a four-step process for overcoming a large gap. The concept of "leveraging your strengths" is explored in depth and guidance is provided to help you apply your unique strengths in new ways that fit the needs of your circumstances.

CHAPTER 9

MAKING A GOOD THING BETTER

MAXIMIZING AN ALREADY GOOD FIT

Reflection without action is an illusion.
Action without reflection is a nightmare.

—Anonymous

At this point, all the pieces are in place for you to apply the Archimedes Principle for Leaders: *Choose the appropriate Leadership Dimension and apply your natural strengths, and you can move your world.* You understand the objectives and tactics for each of the five Leadership Dimensions. You have a solid grasp of your unique strengths and which of the Leadership Dimensions are most natural to you. You have a clear understanding of your particular contextual mix and its requisite Leadership Dimensions. All that remains now is to know how to proceed in your current setting. The answer to that is determined by the "size of your gap."

Here's what we mean: You may already have a general sense of how well your natural strengths in each of the Leadership Dimensions fit current contextual needs—a general sense of the size of the gap between your best performance and the skills required to manage your responsibilities. If the gap between what you do naturally and what is required is quite small, your natural Leadership Dimensions are probably sufficient

—but you may not want to settle for *good enough.* On the other hand, the demands of your context may call for Dimensions that are *not* natural to you—the gap between the skills and knowledge needed and your natural strengths may be quite large. The size of either of these gaps determines the particular strategy needed for implementing the Archimedes Principle. You need one strategy when the gap is small, another when the gap is large.

In the first part of this chapter, you'll determine the size of your gaps in the current setting and see why that matters. The remainder of the chapter suggests strategies on how to *enhance* your effectiveness when the gap is small. The final chapter of the book provides strategies for overcoming a large gap.

HOW BIG IS YOUR GAP?
Comparing What You've Got with What You Need

"All bravery stands on comparisons."

—Sir Francis Bacon, English philosopher

If you aren't quite sure about how your strengths measure up to the demands of your particular context, you will have a *definite* awareness after completing the next exercise.

Tool 18 summarizes the Building Blocks of each of the five Dimensions. Follow the instructions to determine the size of your gap for each Dimension.

Tool 18

CALCULATING THE GAPS

Directions

1. In Tool 17, My Contexts at a Glance, look at the Leadership Dimensions you identified as most needed right now. Circle those Dimensions in the Leadership Dimension column below.
2. Using a scale of 1 to 5, rate your degree of *natural talent* (not developed skill) for each Building Block of the circled Dimensions. Scale: 1 = none, 2 = below average, 3 = average, 4 = above average, 5 = abundant.
3. Tally your total score for each of the circled Dimensions. Subtract your total score from the ideal score to obtain your gap score.

Leadership Dimension	Building Blocks	Strength Rating (Scale of 1–5)
Commanding	■ Quickly determining priorities, based on available information	_____
	■ Making rapid, often unilateral decisions	_____
	■ Issuing clear directives with a brief business rationale	_____
	■ Monitoring for speed of action and compliance	_____
	■ Determining and enforcing consequences for failure to comply	_____
	Ideal Score 20 / My Total Score _____ / **My Gap Score** _____	Total _____
Visioning	■ Formulating with the group a compelling picture of a desirable future	_____
	■ Continually and consistently communicating the vision	_____
	■ Freeing people to take individual and collective action to achieve the vision	_____
	■ Recognizing the contribution of individual and group activities in realizing the vision	_____
	Ideal Score 20 / My Total Score _____ / **My Gap Score** _____	Total _____

continues →

Tool 18 cont'd

Leadership Dimension	Building Blocks	Strength Rating (Scale of 1–5)

Enrolling	▪ Eliciting and genuinely considering input, ideas, and suggestions from group members
	▪ Implementing others' worthwhile ideas
	▪ Publicly crediting others when their ideas, innovations, or improvements are adopted
	▪ Facilitating consensus decision making
	
	        Ideal Score 20
	        My Total Score _____
	        My Gap Score _____
		_____
		_____
		
		_____
		_____
		
		Total
		
		_____

Relating	▪ Caring about the well-being of the whole person, not just what that individual contributes to the organization
	▪ Providing encouragement and emotional support for the individual's or group's efforts
	▪ Mediating conflicts to achieve mutually agreeable resolutions
	▪ Conducting effective teambuilding
	
	        Ideal Score 20
	        My Total Score _____
	        My Gap Score _____
		_____
		
		_____
		
		_____
		_____
		
		Total
		
		_____

Coaching	▪ Assessing strengths, weaknesses, motivations, and potential of individuals and the team
	▪ Providing appropriate "stretch" assignments for professional development
	▪ Ensuring that effective performance feedback is provided
	▪ Using appropriate teaching and training methods for individual/team learning
	▪ Discussing individual career aspirations and plans
	
	        Ideal Score 20
	        My Total Score _____
	        My Gap Score _____
		_____
		
		_____
		
		_____
		
		_____
		_____
		
		Total
		
		_____

DETERMINING THE SIZE OF YOUR GAPS

Now that you have calculated your gap scores, you can determine their significance using a simple classification system. A score of 5 or less indicates a small gap, and a score of 6 or more indicates a large gap. In the chart below, for each of the Leadership Dimensions you selected, record the size of your gap as small or large.

Leadership Dimension   **Size of Gap**

- _____   - _____

- _____   - _____

- _____   - _____

- _____   - _____

The distinction between small and large gaps is important. When the gap is small, it suggests that your use of this Leadership Dimension is easy and effective—it is natural to you. Typically, this Dimension will be one that you identified as being natural to you in Chapter 6.[1] When you use the Building Blocks of such a Dimension, your strategy is simply to enhance your effectiveness, or *up your game.*

When the size of a gap falls into the large range (particularly for scores 12 and higher), it suggests that this Dimension is unnatural to you. Typically, this is a Dimension that you have avoided using or that has created minimal (or even adverse) results. Developing effectiveness in a large-gap Dimension requires a very different strategy, designed to bridge the gap. We will discuss this situation comprehensively in the next chapter.

Before describing our suggested strategies for upping your Leadership Dimension game, we want you to decide if this is actually the best use of your time *at this moment.* If you are facing a context that needs urgent attention and requires the use of a Leadership Dimension that is natural to you and one or more that is not, you would probably be better served by focusing on developing a basic level of effectiveness in the unnatural Dimension, rather than on tweaking your performance in the already strong one. If that is the case, you may want to skip this chapter and proceed to the next. You can return to this chapter when things are less critical. If your context is not so urgent, you may be able to focus on upping your game for a Dimension where the gap is small *and* on bridging the gap in a Dimension where the gap is large.

UPPING YOUR GAME
Strategies for Small Gaps

"Swifter, higher, stronger."

—Motto adopted by the
Olympics, circa 1908

The 1981 Oscar-winning film *Chariots of Fire* carried the tagline: "Two men seeking glory." It told the true story of the 1924 Olympic gold-winning performances of two British sprinters: Eric Liddell, a devout Scottish Christian, and Harold Abrams, the son of a newly rich English Jew. In the film, Abrams is portrayed as pursuing athletic supremacy as a means of proving himself to Cambridge society. In this pursuit, Abrams hires the services of a personal trainer, Sam Mussabini (long before professional coaches were part of the fabric of amateur sports). When interviewing Mussabini, Abrams asks him if he can find another inch in the length of his running stride. After observing Abrams at a competition, Mussabini replies, "I can find you that inch."

Mussabini was not attempting to coach someone who possessed no innate talent for running fast. Abrams was a natural sprinter who had risen to national prominence by virtue of his inborn blazing speed. In finding Abrams another inch in his running stride, Mussabini was simply helping Abrams up his game. He was working with natural talent to enhance an already strong level of performance. It was a matter of tweaking, not transplanting, Abrams's innate abilities.

The same principle is true when you seek to improve your leadership effectiveness in a Dimension for which you possess natural talents and strengths. It's not a question of overcoming poor performance. If this is a Dimension that has only a small gap between the needs of the situation and your strengths (you scored fairly high in each of the related Building Blocks), it's simply a question of upping an already good game. You need only find another inch in your stride to reach even greater levels of success.

Let's take a look at two strategies you can use to up your leadership game.

Strengthening Your Least Developed Building Block

Top professional athletes are naturally talented at all parts of their game. So how do they continue to improve? While continuing to practice and maintain their strongest aspects, they take time out to focus on the part of their game that is the least developed. Working with their natural abilities, they concentrate on tweaking their performance in that area. For instance, a golfer may be strong at all aspects of the game. Nonetheless, his putting game may be relatively underdeveloped in comparison to his other shots. While continuing to practice drives, fairway shots, chip shots, and sand shots, this golfer would also be wise to focus on augmenting his underdeveloped putting game to enhance his overall performance. The same principle holds true when you are using a Dimension for which you possess abundant strengths. You may need to *focus on the part of your game that's the least developed.*

In Tool 18, you rated your current degree of strength in the Building Blocks of the Leadership Dimensions you currently most need to use. Looking at the Leadership Dimensions where your gap is small (you feel quite proficient), you may notice that your score in one of the Building Blocks of that Dimension is lower than the others. If this is the case, you may want to focus on *strengthening that Building Block* to extend your effectiveness in that Dimension. This is particularly important if the Building Block is highly relevant to your current context.

For instance, you may have a small gap score in the Relating Dimension. You may have scored yourself a 3 for mediating conflict and 4s and 5s for the remainder of the specific Building Blocks for that Dimension. If two of your team members are currently involved in a conflict they seem unable to resolve for themselves, it would make sense to focus on tweaking your mediation skills.

Go within every day and find the inner strength so that the world will not blow your candle out.
—Katherine Dunham, dancer

In deciding to strengthen a Building Block, you have to assess whether the relative weakness in that Block is the result of (1) the lack of natural talents for that Building Block, or (2) the lack of opportunity to practice a natural talent you have.

For example, let's say you rated yourself a 2 on the Enrolling Dimension Building Block of facilitating consensus decision making. Does this reflect the absence of a natural strength or a lack of opportunity to develop a latent talent? If you're not sure, try this:

- Reread the full description of this Building Block in Chapter 3

- Review your Strengths-at-a-Glance chart at the end of Chapter 5

- Compare the two to see if your personal strengths naturally lend themselves to the actions required to facilitate consensus decision making (such strengths might include listening effectively to others, clarifying meaning in conversation, reading others' emotions accurately, and being patient with group process)

When You Have the Natural Strengths

If you conclude that in fact you do have the strengths for this Building Block, you will want to create opportunities to practice so you can improve your skill level, from a 2 to a 4. To speed your development, you may also want to obtain performance feedback from your staff after leading a consensus decision-making session. *When you have the natural strengths, you just need the opportunity to practice using them to increase your effectiveness in a particular Building Block.*

When You Lack the Natural Strengths

Let's say you have the natural strengths for this Dimension but lack the natural strengths for one component, facilitating consensus building. You still want or need to use this Building Block, so you'll turn to an important strategy we advocate: *leveraging the strengths you do possess.* In this particular case, it might mean *taking advantage of your self-confidence and humility* and letting a team member more naturally skilled in facilitation lead the process. Or it could involve using your natural task orientation to stress to the group the importance of reaching a mutual decision quickly, while also admitting that at times you may need to be reminded to be patient in letting the group surface a wide variety of options before rushing to choose one to implement. Or it could mean using your natural talent for *envisioning and communicating a desired future* to create enthusiasm for the consensus-building process, even while you remind team members that your strength is not in facilitation and that you will need their help in the process. These are just a few ways that existing strengths can be leveraged into a Building Block.

The keys to leveraging your strengths are (1) knowing clearly what your natural strengths are, and (2) finding ways to use those strengths in the situation. If you initially find it difficult to do this on your own, you may want to secure the assistance of a coach until you become more proficient at seeing how your strengths can be applied. Our Web site (www.5DLeadership.com) contains the needed information to find a coach who can assist you in this regard.

To summarize, the first strategy for dealing with a small gap is to strengthen your weaker Building Block. Here are the steps:

1. Review the description of the Building Block (Chapter 3)

2. Review your natural strengths listed in your Strengths at a Glance chart (page 118)

3. Compare the two to see if your strengths are a natural fit for that Building Block

4. Practice using the Building Block when you have the natural strengths for it, or leverage other strengths into it when you do not

Extending Your Reach

The second strategy for dealing with a small gap is to *extend your reach.* This involves looking for new areas in which to use a Leadership Dimension. This strategy is valuable when you have one or more "high-strength" Leadership Dimensions. These are Dimensions in which you have abundant strength in all the Building Blocks. In other words, the gap between the "ideal" and your performance is *very small.* While it's always possible to refine your performance in a particular Dimension, you do need to determine if making further adjustments will bring further significant improvements. If not, it might be wiser to extend your reach by looking for new areas in which to use this Leadership Dimension. In an organizational setting, extending your reach involves (1) heightening your awareness of environments or situations where you can use this Leadership Dimension, and (2) offering or choosing to lead in those arenas.

What does this look like in practice?

Exercising Ad Hoc Leadership

At times this strategy involves *assuming leadership on a short-term, ad hoc basis to deal with a one-time event or immediate need.* Occasionally this involves situations that, while technically falling under a colleague's area of responsibility, nonetheless require an *immediate* response. In these circumstances it is usually appropriate simply to act without first checking with your colleague. For example, if you are very strong in the Relating Dimension, it would be wise to step in and use this Dimension with a customer who has become extremely angry and is on the verge of becoming violent or abusive toward an employee. The fact that that employee is not in your department or is managed by someone else is irrelevant. Certainly in cases where someone else has formal authority over the situation, you should consider whether you are overstepping your bounds and *inappropriately* encroaching on someone else's area of responsibility. The degree to which immediate action is needed is usually the deciding factor.

These "emergency" situations are relatively infrequent. More common are situations where a colleague or your boss has little or no natural talent for the Leadership Dimension required by the circumstances and you do. In these circumstances, you may want to offer to lead on their behalf. For example, let's say Tom has a high-strength Coaching Dimension. He is on the executive team for a company that is growing and consequently needs to promote someone into a newly created VP role. The person offered the position is currently a direct report of one of Tom's colleagues and has some leadership development needs that could be addressed quickly through effective coaching. In a situation like this, it might be appropriate and beneficial to the organization for Tom to extend his reach and offer to coach the new VP.

When deciding whether to offer the use of a Leadership Dimension in a situation that is someone else's formal responsibility, you must gauge how that offer will be interpreted. If the relationship between you and the person to whom you are offering your leadership strength is strong—characterized by mutual trust, openness, and respect—it is usually appropriate. If the relationship is not strong, offering to lead may be perceived as suggesting that you consider the person to be incompetent or that you are seeking to aggrandize yourself at his or her expense. In such cases, it's usually not worth offering, given the negative repercussions that the offer may create.

So the first means of extending your reach with a "small-gap Dimension" is to exercise leadership on a short-term, ad hoc basis to deal with a one-time event or immediate need.

Seeking New Assignments

The other means is to seek out new, longer-term responsibilities that particularly require that Leadership Dimension. Special projects or longer-term assignments often call for a "specialization" in one or more of the Leadership Dimensions, and if it is a high-strength Dimension for you, it may be advantageous (both for the company and for you) to seek the opportunity. For example, let's say your company is about to begin negotiations on a new collective agreement with the union that represents your employees. You know that you are very strong in the Enrolling Dimension. You might offer to become a key player or even the leader of the management negotiation team, a setting that would require extensive use of this Dimension, particularly the facilitating consensus decision making Building Block. Alternatively, you might have tremendous strength in the Relating Dimension. Management-union negotiations could also be an environment that would capitalize on Relating—particularly in conflict resolution and building trust. The key is to look for and take advantage of longer-term projects or assignments that allow you to capitalize on your high-strength Leadership Dimensions.

If you are going to choose to extend your reach by seeking longer-term responsibilities, you will likely need to divest yourself of some current responsibilities. This can be accomplished in two ways. If you have a strong team atmosphere and your colleagues understand the organizational benefits of letting you specialize in an area of high strength, you may be able to distribute your current responsibilities among your peers. The other way to create space for new responsibilities is to delegate some of your current ones to key subordinates. This often serves as a means of development for them as well.

To summarize, the second strategy for dealing with a small gap is to extend your reach—looking for new areas in which to use a Leadership Dimension. This is particularly relevant for high-strength Leadership Dimensions and can be achieved in two ways:

1. Assuming leadership on a short-term, ad hoc basis to deal with a one-time event or immediate need

2. Seeking out new, longer-term responsibilities that particularly require that Dimension

CONCLUSION

The size of the gap between the ideal level of strength for a Leadership Dimension and what you actually possess has a significant bearing on how you proceed to use that Dimension. This chapter has focused on using a Dimension where the gap is small. In such a case, it is a matter of upping your game, either strengthening a weaker Building Block in that Dimension or extending the use of a high-strength Dimension into new areas.

The much more significant challenge involves using a Dimension where the gap is large. Mastering that challenge is the topic of our final chapter.

CHAPTER 10

YOU DON'T HAVE TO TAKE A FLYING LEAP

BRIDGING A LARGE GAP

Your problem is to bridge the gap which exists between where you are now and the goal you intend to reach.

—Earl Nightingale, broadcaster

Bridging the gap is what we're about here. You know how to enhance a strong fit between the strengths you already have and the Leadership Dimensions a situation requires. This chapter provides a strategy for overcoming the challenge when you need to use a certain Leadership Dimension yet possess few, if any, natural strengths in that area.

BUILDING A BRIDGE
What to Do When the Gap Is Large

The wise man bridges the gap by laying out the path by means of which he can get from where he is to where he wants to go.

—J.P. Morgan

What is a leader to do when the gap between a needed Leadership Dimension and his or her natural strengths is large? There are really only two options for crossing the gap. The first is to take a flying leap. This equates to exerting tremendous effort and trying to transform your weaknesses into strengths. This is the traditional approach to leadership development, and as we argued earlier, typically the results fall far short of the mark. The good news is that there is a second, far better way to cross the divide: by building a bridge.

The process for building a bridge to cross the Leadership Dimensions gap involves four distinct steps:

1. Know your destination

2. Build the bridge

3. Cross the bridge

4. Don't look back

The remainder of this chapter details these steps.

Know Your Destination

The process of bridging a large Leadership Dimensions gap begins by clarifying which specific Leadership Dimensions and Building Blocks are most relevant in your context (see Chapter 3 for a review of these). Not all Building Blocks related to a Dimension are necessarily relevant to your circumstances, and those that are relevant will vary in importance. Identifying and prioritizing these Building Blocks is the first step in bridging a large gap, preparing a leader to determine which particular strengths he or she can best leverage.

To illustrate, let's say Martha, a CEO, has determined that in order to stay competitive in the industry, her business needs to make a fundamental shift in its corporate culture, moving from a slower-paced, hierarchical, bureaucratic structure to a faster, team-oriented, decentralized approach. Considering this objective, she knows that she is going to need to rely heavily on the Visioning Dimension during this change initiative, a Dimension that is not at all natural to her.

As she reviews the Building Blocks of the Visioning Dimension from Chapter 3, she decides that all four Building Blocks of this Dimension will be needed:

- Formulating with the group a compelling picture of a desirable future

- Continually and consistently communicating the vision

- Freeing people to take individual and collective action to achieve the vision

- Recognizing the contribution of individual and group activities in realizing the vision

However, Martha also decides that given the nature of the transition—moving from a centralized, bureaucratic structure to a more empowered, decentralized one—the third and fourth Building Blocks are particularly important. In fact, these two Building Blocks are at the heart of the cultural shift that needs to take place. Her employees have had long years of being schooled in and rewarded for complying with directives, deferring to authority, and strictly following the numerous company policies and procedures. A change toward strongly supporting and rewarding local, team, and individual initiative will be critical in achieving a lasting transition. Thus, Martha realizes that although the first two Building Blocks are important and have *chronological* priority, what will really be crucial to the success of this change initiative is employing Building Blocks 3 and 4 well.

> *I can't change the direction of the wind, but I can adjust my sails to always reach my destination.*
>
> —*Jimmy Dean, actor*

This is the process a leader goes through in this first step of bridging a large gap. Now it's your turn. See Tool 19.

The first step, knowing your destination, is now complete: you know the specific Building Blocks you will need to use to be effective. Now you need to determine how to use your existing strengths to build the bridge across the gap.

Tool 19

IDENTIFYING YOUR BUILDING BLOCKS

Directions: Take a moment to review Tool 18, "Determining the Size of Your Gaps." Based on your scores, which Dimension involves a large gap (a score of 6 or more)? List this Dimension here. If you have more than one "large-gap Dimension," record all of them.

1. _____

2. _____

3. _____

Next review the Building Blocks from Chapter 3 for the Leadership Dimensions you identified. Record in order of importance the ones that are most relevant to achieving your objectives.

Prioritized List of Building Blocks You Need to Employ:

1. _____

2. _____

3. _____

4. _____

5. _____

Finally, put an asterisk (*) beside the Building Blocks you think will prove the greatest challenge to you.

Build the Bridge

Here is a problem for you to try to solve:

A man is replacing a wheel on his car when he accidentally drops the four nuts used to hold the wheel on the car, and they fall into a deep drain, irretrievably lost. A passing girl offers him a solution that enables him to drive home. What is it?

The answer is to use one nut from each of the other three wheels. This problem, and its solution, parallels the challenge leaders experience when they need to use a Leadership Dimension for which they possess few natural strengths. The best solution is to "borrow nuts from the other wheels." In other words, apply your *existing* strengths in *new ways* to use the Building Blocks your circumstances require. Leveraging your strengths is the key to building a bridge over a large Leadership Dimensions gap.

> *We're all pilgrims on the same journey—but some pilgrims have better road maps.*
> —Nelson Demille, author

Recognizing how to apply your existing strengths in new ways often requires *lateral thinking*, a term coined by Edward de Bono.[1] He defines it as a problem-solving technique that approaches problems from a number of different angles instead of concentrating at length on one approach. Lateral thinking requires us to check our assumptions and look for unexpected solutions; it was required to solve the puzzle above.

De Bono identifies four critical factors associated with lateral thinking:

- Recognizing dominant ideas that polarize perception of a problem
- Searching for novel ways of looking at things
- Relaxing rigid control of thinking
- Using chance to encourage other ideas; this last factor has to do with the fact that lateral thinking involves low-probability ideas that are unlikely to occur in the normal course of events

In terms of leveraging your strengths, these four factors translate as

- Recognizing the typical ways you employ your strengths
- Looking for ways to apply these same strengths using the Building Blocks of a different Dimension
- Relaxing your views on the "right" way to use these strengths
- Using brainstorming and other creative thinking techniques[2] to explore possibilities, no matter how silly or impractical they seem at first

Lateral thinking requires a certain flexible mind-set, which some individuals seem to access readily, but most of us need to learn this process over time. To get a sense of how readily this type of thinking comes to you (or doesn't), try to solve the following problems. Answers are on page 221.

Lateral Thinking Problem #1
A woman had two sons who were born on the same hour of the same day of the same year. But they were not twins, and they were not adopted. How could this be so?

Lateral Thinking Problem #2
Three switches outside a windowless room are connected to three light bulbs inside the room. How can you determine which switch is connected to which bulb if you are allowed to enter the room only once?

Lateral Thinking Problem #3
If you put a small coin into an empty wine bottle and replace the cork, how can you get the coin out of the bottle without taking out the cork or breaking the bottle?

Don't be discouraged if you found these problems difficult. Lateral thinking develops with practice. So let's keep practicing.

Here are two scenarios that will allow you to try using lateral thinking in terms of leveraging one's strengths. Jot down your answers in the space below each scenario. Our suggestions are recorded on pages 221–222.

Leveraging Strengths Scenario #1
Amanda needs to use the Commanding Dimension to deal with a difficult employee. Specifically, her circumstances require her to use these two Building Blocks:

- Issuing clear directives with a brief business rationale
- Monitoring for compliance and enforcing consequences for noncompliance

These are some of Amanda's strengths:

- Being enthusiastic
- Being warmhearted
- Identifying with other people's feelings
- Listening to understand others' meaning
- Showing tact when dealing with people

How might Amanda use these strengths with the Commanding Building Blocks she needs to use?

Scenario #1

_____

_____

_____

_____

_____

Leveraging Strengths Scenario #2

Gerry needs to use the following Coaching Building Blocks to develop the leadership capacity of one of his direct reports:

- Providing appropriate "stretch" assignments for professional development
- Ensuring that effective performance feedback takes place

These are some of Gerry's strengths:

- Confronting problems quickly and directly
- Being objective and systematic in analyzing problems
- Being candid in communicating information

- Categorizing information usefully
- Having great factual recall

How might Gerry use these strengths with the Coaching Building Blocks he needs to use?

Scenario #2

_____

_____

_____

_____

_____

Now that you have had a chance to practice lateral thinking with regard to applying someone else's strengths, it's time to do this for yourself. If you still feel like you need more ideas on how to do this, we suggest that you reread Bill's and Daniel's stories in Chapter 4. Tool 20 will help you determine how to take advantage of your strengths in employing the Building Blocks your circumstances require.

As you attempt to complete this step of the bridge-building process, keep in mind that lateral thinking is more an art than a science. It develops with practice. Some people find that thinking laterally works best in consultation with another individual rather than on their own. It may be in your best interest to ask a trusted friend or adviser to brainstorm with you when practicing lateral thinking with regard to leveraging your strengths. Alternatively, you could secure the services of a coach who understands the "leveraging your strengths" approach and who can help you learn this type of lateral thought process. You can check out our Web site for details on how to find a coach to help you in this process: www.5DLeadership.com.

Determining how to leverage your strengths creates a bridge across the Leadership Dimensions gap. Now you need to cross over to the other side.

Tool 20

LEVERAGING YOUR STRENGTHS

Directions:
1. Transfer into the first section below your list of strengths from page 118.
2. Transfer your list of prioritized Building Blocks from page 208 to the pages that follow (one Building Block per page).
3. In Column A, choose from your list of strengths, those you think would be applicable for each Building Block.
4. In Column B, describe possible concrete applications of those strengths.

Strengths from My Strengths at a Glance Chart:

1. _____
2. _____
3. _____
4. _____
5. _____
6. _____
7. _____
8. _____
9. _____
10. _____
11. _____
12. _____
13. _____
14. _____
15. _____

continues →

Tool 20 cont'd

Building Block:

_____

_____

_____

Column A
Strengths That I Could
Apply to this Building Block

Column B
Possible Applications
of these Strengths

- _____

- _____

- _____

- _____

- _____

- _____

- _____

- _____

- _____

- _____

Building Block:

_____

_____

_____

Column A
Strengths That I Could
Apply to this Building Block

Column B
Possible Applications
of these Strengths

- _____
- _____
- _____
- _____
- _____
- _____

- _____
  _____
- _____
  _____
- _____
  _____
- _____
  _____
- _____
  _____
- _____
  _____

continues →

Tool 20 cont'd

Building Block:

_____

_____

_____

Column A Strengths That I Could Apply to this Building Block	Column B Possible Applications of these Strengths
▪ _____	▪ _____
	_____
▪ _____	▪ _____
	_____
▪ _____	▪ _____
	_____
▪ _____	▪ _____
	_____
▪ _____	▪ _____
	_____
▪ _____	▪ _____
	_____

Building Block:

_____

_____

_____

Column A
Strengths That I Could
Apply to this Building Block

Column B
Possible Applications
of these Strengths

- _____
- _____

- _____
- _____

- _____
- _____

- _____
- _____

- _____
- _____

- _____
- _____

continues →

Tool 20 cont'd

Building Block:

_____

_____

_____

Column A
Strengths That I Could
Apply to this Building Block

Column B
Possible Applications
of these Strengths

- _____

- _____

- _____

- _____

- _____

- _____

- _____

- _____

- _____

- _____

- _____

- _____

Cross the Bridge

Now that you have determined applications of your strengths for the Building Blocks you need to use, the time has come to act. As you attempt to use your strengths in these Building Blocks, here are some points to keep in mind.

- Expect your initial attempts to be less than perfect. The fact that you are relying on a strength does not mean that you will use it with skill when you first apply it in a new context. It does suggest that you should be able to learn to use it skillfully quite rapidly. This is the primary advantage of leveraging strengths rather than trying to overcome weaknesses.

- You will need to evaluate your effectiveness on a regular basis. This point is the corollary of the first. Monitoring your effectiveness is the means by which you can recognize and overcome initial stumbles in your attempt to cross the bridge. Keep in mind that effectiveness is determined by the outcomes of your actions, not your degree of comfort while acting.

- The best way to evaluate effectiveness is to get feedback from those whom you are leading. While you should observe the impact your actions are having on the circumstances and the people involved, obtaining feedback from those who are experiencing your leadership is the best means of judging your effectiveness. Granted, this takes a degree of trust and openness and if your staff are not used to being this candid with you, they may at first be reluctant to be fully honest with you. Persist in asking for their honest feedback, be appreciative, and don't react negatively if they indicate that your effectiveness has been less than stellar.

- It may be useful to have a coach to help you learn to use your strengths in these new ways. Having someone who is professionally trained to observe your actions and provide insightful feedback can speed learning immensely.

Using these guidelines, you should quickly develop skills in leveraging your strengths to achieve high levels of effectiveness in your new

Leadership Dimensions. You will have crossed the Leadership Dimensions gap. Now you need to make sure you stay on the other side.

Don't Look Back

> *They say it takes 21 consecutive days to form a new habit. It takes only a moment to break a new habit and revert to the old way of doing things.*
>
> —Anne Toner Fung, Adao Institute for Change

As Anne Toner Fung points out, it is easy to revert to old ways, particularly under stress. A wise leader will be alert for signs of regression to old habits and ways of thinking. This requires regular times of reflection when you are trying to learn new behaviors. It is also wise to ask others to look for such regression and give you feedback. In time, the new behaviors will become rooted in new neural pathways and will be self-sustaining. But this does take time and consistency of new behaviors. To quote Fung further, "To sustain . . . change, we have to make sure that positive reinforcement of the new habit continues long after the initial change has been fully implemented. In fact, we must continue to reinforce the new habit until it becomes easier, more familiar and more comfortable than the old way of doing things."[3]

Again, having a mentor or professional coach can be of great assistance in reinforcing new behaviors. In fact, coaching is an integral aspect of our leadership development programs. Having someone who will encourage us to maintain our new behaviors, celebrate with us our successes, and tell us when we are reverting to old behaviors helps us overcome the pull of old habits and our tendency to be blind to our mistakes.

CONCLUSION

In many ways, this final chapter has been the most important one of the book. It goes to the heart of our approach to leadership development: leveraging your strengths while employing the Leadership Dimensions required by your context.

The challenge of leading well in the real world is immense. We have attempted to be as practical as possible in giving you the perspectives and tools needed to rise to the challenge. We hope your motivation level is high to translate your intention into action. The epilogue will give you a process and a tool for making concrete plans to implement what you have learned.

Answers to Lateral Thinking Problems

Lateral Thinking Problem #1
They were two of a set of triplets (or quadruplets or . . .)

Lateral Thinking Problem #2
Switch on the first switch, leave it for a minute, and then switch it off again. Then switch on the second switch and enter the room. The second switch will be connected to the light that is on, the first switch will be connected to the light with the warm bulb, and the third switch will be connected to the light with the cold bulb.

Lateral Thinking Problem #3
Push the cork into the bottle and then tip the bottle over and dump out the coin.

Our Solutions for the Leveraging Your Strengths Scenarios

Leveraging Your Strengths Scenario #1
Amanda's strengths could serve her well when she first meets with her staff member to confront the problem behavior. Amanda's sensitivity to others' emotions will help her anticipate how this particular staff member will respond emotionally to being given "an ultimatum." She can use this knowledge to prepare how she will frame the issue so as to minimize resistance. Her warmth and tact will help in making the message of "comply or else" more palatable. Amanda can use her listening skills to make sure her employee feels heard and to make sure that she has not misunderstood anything in the situation that might affect her approach. Her enthusiasm can be an asset in communicating the importance of the business rationales for the behavior she requires from her employee and when asking her employee to comply with these requirements.

Should it become necessary to discipline her staff member, her warmth, tact, and understanding of others' feelings can help her speak and behave in a way that will minimize (though not eliminate) a strong negative emotional reaction to the enforcement of consequences.

Leveraging Your Strengths Scenario #2

Gerry's strengths can be leveraged very effectively for coaching. He can certainly use his categorizing abilities to define precisely the requirements of the leadership role for which he is preparing his direct report. Furthermore, his talent for objective and systematic analysis will be very useful in assessing his direct report's current strengths and weaknesses regarding the upcoming leadership role. Together, these strengths should help Gerry determine assignments that will provide the appropriate amount of stretch for his direct report.

Gerry's tendency to confront problems quickly and directly, combined with both his analytical abilities and his candidness in communication could serve to provide specific, concrete, objective feedback that will help his staff member clearly understand what is going well and what still needs to be improved. As the coaching continues, his factual recall will help him provide specific examples of how his direct report's actions have improved over time.

EPILOGUE

ACTIONS SPEAK LOUDER THAN WORDS

A good plan is like a road map: it shows the final destination and usually the best way to get there.

—H. Stanley Judd, author

Throughout this book we have given you the opportunity to interact with our concepts by means of various activities. What remains now is to give you a chance to create a more comprehensive plan of action for your leadership development.

Tool 21 provides an opportunity to map out your personal action plan. Before completing it, you might want to review the content of this book, looking for key insights, learning activities and exercises you didn't complete at the time, and actions you now need to take. Acting on these while the concepts are fresh in your mind is critical to making your development effective.

Tool 21

MY PERSONAL LEADERSHIP DEVELOPMENT ACTION PLAN

Directions: Record the insights you've gained from this book, the activities you need to complete, and the action steps you need to take in the space provided.

Key Insights I Have Gained

- _____
- _____
- _____
- _____
- _____

Learning Activities I Still Need to Complete

- _____
- _____
- _____
- _____
- _____

Action Steps I Need to Take	To Be Completed By	Completed? Yes/No
_____	_____	_____
_____	_____	_____
_____	_____	_____
_____	_____	_____
_____	_____	_____

CONCLUSION

One final suggestion: You may want to include as part of your action plan a commitment to teaching these ideas to others. Few things solidify our understanding of a concept better than having to teach it to someone else.

We encourage you to return frequently to this book as a guide in your ongoing leadership development. We would enjoy hearing from you if you have questions or comments or want to share examples of how the ideas in the book have enhanced your leadership effectiveness. You can contact us at info@5DLeadership.com.

APPENDIX A

THE PREVALENCE OF COMMAND AND CONTROL

Why do so many leaders rely so heavily (some, exclusively) on the Commanding Dimension of leadership?

Two particular reasons account for that Dimension's prevalence. The first reason is that the Commanding approach to leadership is a natural, perhaps inevitable, outgrowth of the two most common mental models used to typify organizations: the military and the machine.

Until recently, most organizations modeled themselves explicitly after the hierarchical structure of the military. Many still do. Military metaphors, terms, and jargon still abound in organizational and business conversation and communiqués. Phrases like "the company's commander-in-chief," "my generals," "winning the war," and "establishing a beach-head" abound. Business books that extol and model the successes of military leaders remain popular. A recent example is the book *Business as War: Battling for Competitive Advantage* by Kenneth Allard. Allard is a former army colonel and well-known commentator on international security issues, strategy, and military matters. His chapter "Building Leaders of Character" contains a discussion of ten lessons of military leadership, one of which is "Command & Control Is Good: Self-Control Is Even Better." Military leadership, whether by Kenneth Allard, Sun-Tzu, the ancient Chinese military genius, or General Colin Powell, is often lionized and copied by today's business leaders. Since Commanding is the standard Leadership Dimension used in the military (though, even there, this is changing; see Mike Abrashoff's story in Chapter 2), it seems natural for many business leaders to adopt it as the primary, if not exclusive, leadership style in business.

A second widespread organizational metaphor is that of the machine. This mechanistic perception of organizational structure and dynamics has led to attempts by executives and managers to control,

227

regulate, and predict all aspects of the business, including its workforce. Individual workers are often treated as virtually interchangeable parts of a complex machine. Emotion and passion are seen as disruptive forces, interfering with the smooth flow of work. Emphasis is put on managing the processes of the work, not motivating and inspiring people to be fully engaged. True ownership of the job by the staff member is typically seen as too risky a proposition or "emotional gobbledygook" that is irrelevant to the bottom line. What is needed, it is believed, is simply for people to do what they are told. These assumptions, beliefs, and practices emerge naturally from the "organization as machine" framework and clearly fit the command-and-control style of leadership.

These two metaphors (the military and the machine) mutually reinforce each other and have led to the prioritization and common practice of the Commanding Dimension of leadership. Most of today's senior leaders have grown up with these mental models, which are deeply imbedded. Consequently, many of them tend to rely heavily on the Commanding Dimension—even when they know better. It flows from their framework. That is the first reason why this style is so common.

A second reason is the seductiveness of the Commanding Dimension. Quite simply, this mode of leading others can appear easier and may provide more ego strokes than other ways of leading. Issuing directives rather than trusting your associates often feels safer and can make you feel important. Disregarding the messy world of feelings and relationships can seem attractive, especially when you aren't used to having to deal with emotions at work and see them as irrelevant to getting the job done. Making the key decisions yourself rather than building consensus is certainly faster and assures that your priorities and preferences prevail. Believing that you can control the factors you deem essential to succeed certainly feels empowering. This is the seductiveness of the Commanding Dimension, and a second powerful factor in explaining its prevalence.

CONTRASTING MANAGEMENT AND LEADERSHIP

The contrast between leadership and management is one that has been drawn for some time now, but it is still often misunderstood or ignored. Furthermore, some of the discussion of the difference tends to downplay the importance of managing, as if it is a lesser task than leading. In our experience, the most effective executives, middle managers, and supervisors have developed both their management and leadership abilities. Both are necessary for long-term success. Yet many executives are much more experienced with managing than leading. Consequently, they end up achieving far less than if they practiced both management and leadership in their roles.

The chart that follows highlights some of the differences between managing and leading. As will be seen, managing and leading are actions not positions, functions not titles. Whatever one's formal title, *both* managing and leading are required to be fully effective.

	WHEN MANAGING	WHEN LEADING
Focus	Processes and procedures	People and possibilities
Goal	Efficiency—doing things best	Effectiveness—doing the best things
Priority	Maximizing the efficiency of the current systems and processes	Turning the vision of the future into a current reality
Time Orientation	Past, present, and immediate future	Present, immediate future, and distant future
Relies Most On	▪ Planning ▪ Monitoring ▪ Coordinating	▪ Relating ▪ Modeling ▪ Inspiring
Staff Members Are Seen As	Resources to be allocated in meeting current objectives and needs of the business	Resources to be developed in realizing the future potential of the business
Desired Response from Staff	Complete compliance with the organization's standards and procedures	Whole hearted commitment to the organization's vision and values
Orientation to Status Quo	Accepts and refines it to achieve specified targets	Challenges and changes it to align with the mission and the vision
Communication Style	▪ Objective ▪ Rational ▪ Detailed ▪ Informative ▪ Transactional	▪ Inspirational ▪ Intuitive ▪ Visionary ▪ Persuasive ▪ Transformational
Defines Success As	▪ Meeting standards and deadlines ▪ Maintaining quality ▪ Smooth functioning of processes	▪ Commitment to the mission and values ▪ Innovative improvements in quality ▪ Developing new ways to realize the vision
Core Dimensions Include	▪ Planning ▪ Organizing ▪ Supervising ▪ Delegating ▪ Standardizing	▪ Commanding ▪ Visioning ▪ Enrolling ▪ Relating ▪ Coaching

FOUR RECOMMENDED FORMAL ASSESSMENT TOOLS

The four assessments we discuss here are all excellent tools. Choose the ones you think will benefit you the most.

MYERS-BRIGGS TYPE INDICATOR® (MBTI®) ASSESSMENT

The *Myers-Briggs Type Indicator®* (MBTI®) assessment is the most widely used personality inventory in the world. It was developed by Isabel Briggs Myers and Katharine Cook Briggs and is based on the personality type theory of Carl Jung, a Swiss psychiatrist of the early twentieth century. The MBTI assessment sorts individuals into one of sixteen psychological types, based on a pattern of preferred mental processes. Understanding your psychological type provides several valuable leadership insights, including

- General themes in how you prefer to lead others

- Your preferred manner of problem solving

- How you express your creativity as a leader

- Your natural contributions to a leadership team

- Your personal leadership stressors and their antidotes

- Your preferred learning style

- A general path for your leadership development

FIRO-B® INSTRUMENT

The FIRO-B® instrument assesses how your personal needs influence your leadership behaviors with others. It is based on the assumption that all human interactions are influenced by three factors:

- **The need for inclusion**—the extent of contact and prominence that a person needs in relationships

- **The need for control**—the extent of power or dominance a person seeks in decision making, influence, and persuasion

- **The need for affection**—the extent of emotional closeness a person seeks with others

Each of these three factors is assessed in two Dimensions: the extent to which you initiate a particular behavior with those you lead, and the extent to which you desire that same behavior from others.

Understanding your pattern of relationship needs provides several valuable leadership insights:

- Your pattern of fulfilling your inclusion, control, and affection needs

- The roles you prefer to take on within an organization

- How you work in a leadership team setting

- What you expect from other leaders

- Your preferred bases of power and influence

- Which Dimension (inclusion, control, or affection) you show first in a leadership role

A Leadership Report is available that ties together the results of your MBTI and FIRO-B profiles.

BARON EMOTIONAL QUOTIENT INVENTORY®

For several years now, the concept of emotional intelligence has been gaining acceptance as a framework that explains who succeeds in life and why. Emotional intelligence explores your awareness of and ability to manage your own and others' emotions. It is becoming recognized as more significant than mental intelligence or technical competence in determining success and excellence at work, especially for leaders. Daniel Goleman's books in particular have made the findings of this field accessible and relevant to organizational leaders.

Several instruments exist for assessing your current level of emotional intelligence. The original, and one of the most widely tested, is the *BarOn Emotional Quotient Inventory®*. It explores your strengths in five dimensions:

- **Intrapersonal**—self-regard, emotional self-awareness, assertiveness, independence, and self-actualization

- **Interpersonal**—empathy, social responsibility, interpersonal relationships

- **Adaptability**—reality testing, flexibility, and problem solving

- **Stress Management**—stress tolerance and impulse control

- **General Mood**—optimism and happiness

These dimensions have numerous implications for one's current effectiveness as a leader. For example, while I may possess a personal strength of meticulous attention to detail, how I employ that strength will be greatly influenced by my general degree of optimism or pessimism. The pessimistic leader may use it to constantly check up on staff, assuming things are bound to go wrong without such micromanagement. The optimistic leader may use it to create detailed plans to carry out a bold vision for the future.

THE LEADERSHIP CIRCLE PROFILE

The Leadership Circle Profile (TLCP) uses a 360° feedback process to measure an individual's effectiveness in two primary leadership domains:

- **Creative Competencies**—the positive aspects of leadership, such as how you achieve results, bring out the best in others, lead with vision, enhance your own development, act with integrity and courage, and improve organizational systems

- **Reactive Tendencies**—negative leadership styles that emphasize caution over creating results, self-protection over productive engagement, and aggression over building alignment; these self-limiting styles overemphasize the focus on gaining the approval of others, protecting yourself, and getting results through high control tactics

TLCP explores the internal assumptions (beliefs) that influence behavior in both domains. This allows the individual to see how his or her inner world of thought is translating into a productive or unproductive style of leadership. Ultimately this profile increases the inner awareness that affects outward behavior.

TLCP displays results within a high-impact framework, not merely in the rank-order scores found in most surveys. Its high-impact framework springs from the best models of adult development. This framework both shows leaders how they are doing and spotlights the hidden motivators that drive successful and unsuccessful behavior.

TWO CAUTIONS WHEN USING THESE TOOLS

First, there is no magic or science in these instruments that makes them infallible. It is the nature of all self-report instruments, no matter how well constructed or rigorously validated, that they can only convey the results of what you actually indicate. Your responses to particular items are a reflection of your current level of self-awareness. However, as we discussed earlier in this book, there are many aspects of ourselves of which we are unaware. In selecting a particular response, you may actually be indicating something about yourself that is neither characteristic nor accurate. The instrument has no power to determine if your response really is true of you; it can only report back the implications of what you selected. Treat the results of any self-report instrument as information to be considered, not as absolute truth.

Second, you will need to find someone who is qualified to administer, score, and interpret the results for you. Be careful whom you choose. There are many individuals who have received their certification to purchase and administer these tools, but that doesn't mean they are all highly skilled at interpreting the results or even understanding the depths of the theory on which the instrument is based. Furthermore, a good facilitator will lead you through a self-validation process and will also help you make the most of the information contained in the report. Beware of those who simply announce the results to you without guiding you to validate the results for yourself. If you would like to receive suggestions on whom to contact in your area to administer and interpret your results, please contact us at our Web site: info@5DLeadership.com.

In concluding this review of formal assessment instruments, we stress once more the importance of finding well-qualified individuals to administer the instrument and interpret the results. It is worth the time it takes to find a good facilitator so you can maximize the benefits of these assessment instruments.

NOTES

CHAPTER 1

1. *Newsweek,* 2003.
2. Nancy Gibbs, "Person of the Year," *Time,* December 31, 2001, *158*(28).
3. Jimmy Carter for President 1976, campaign brochure, "For American's third century, why not our best?"
4. Fred I. Greenstein, *The Presidential Difference: Leadership Style from FDR to Clinton* (New York: Free Press, 2000), 128–129.
5. Rogers Wilkins, as quoted in "Carter's 'Crisis of Confidence' Speech," PBS article related to *The American Experience.*
6. Interview with Professor Douglas Brinkley on *Talking History,* November 19, 1998. www.albany.edu/talkinghistory/arch98july-december.html.
7. As quoted in Margot Morrell and Stephanie Capparell, *Shackleton's Way: Leadership Lessons from the Great Antarctic Explorer* (New York: Penguin Putnam, 2001), 61.
8. Morrell and Capparell, *Shackleton's Way,* 56.
9. Caroline Alexander, *The Endurance: Shackleton's Legendary Antarctic Expedition* (New York: Alfred A. Knopf), 56.
10. Morrell and Capparell, *Shackleton's Way,* 133.
11. Alexander, *The Endurance,* 93.
12. Ibid., 119.
13. Ibid., 127.

CHAPTER 2

1. Implicit in our definition of leadership is a distinction between managing and leading. Both are necessary for organizational success. Appendix B offers a comprehensive description of the distinction between these two aspects of the managerial role.
2. "More Than a Motorcycle: The Leadership Journey at Harley-Davidson." A conversation with Rich Teerlink and Lee Ozley. *HBS Working Knowledge,* September 5, 2000. www.hbsworkingknowledge.hbs.edu/item.jhtml?id=1677&t=leadership.
3. Peter M. Senge, "Communities of Leaders and Learners," *Harvard Business Review,* September–October 1997, 30.
4. "More Than a Motorcycle."

5. Jan Carlzon, *Moments of Truth* (New York: Harper Perennial, 1987), 27.
6. Ibid., 18.
7. Ibid.
8. Richard Teerlink, "Harley's Leadership U-Turn," *Harvard Business Review*, July–August 2000, Product No. R00411, p. 5.
9. Ibid.
10. Ibid.
11. Ibid.
12. D. Michael Abrashoff, *It's Your Ship: Management Techniques from the Best Damn Ship in the Navy* (New York: Warner Books, 2004).
13. Polly Labarre, "The Agenda—Grassroots Leadership," *Fast Company*, April 1999, Issue 23, 114.
14. Mike Abrashoff, "Retention Through Redemption." www.grassrootsleadership.com.
15. Ibid.
16. As quoted in Labarre, "The Agenda—Grassroots Leadership."
17. D. Michael Abrashoff, "Retention Through Redemption," *Harvard Business Review*, February 2001, Product No. R0102L, 6.

CHAPTER 3

1. James C. Collins and Jerry I. Porras, "Organizational Vision and Visionary Organizations," *California Management Review*, Fall 1991, *34*.
2. Peter Jensen, *Coaching for High Performance*, audio program (Rockwood, Ont.: Performance Coaching, 2000).
3. From Giro Sports Design's corporate vision statement as quoted by Collins and Porras in "Organizational Vision and Visionary Organizations."
4. Warren Bennis and Joan Goldsmith, *Learning to Lead* (Cambridge, Mass.: Perseus Books, 1997), 100.
5. John P. Kotter, *Leading Change* (Boston: Harvard Business School Press, 1996), 101–115.
6. Recent research by the Gallup Organization defines the twelve most important factors in creating fully engaged employees. Number four on the list states, "In the last seven days, I have received recognition or praise for good work." This finding (employees' desire for regular, genuine recognition) is consistent with virtually all research findings on employee motivation over the last several decades. But the Gallup research has been able to quantify how frequently such recognition needs to be given. It turns out that most employees need it at least weekly. Marcus Buckingham and Curt Coffman, *First Break All the Rules: What the World's Greatest Managers Do Differently* (New York: Simon & Schuster, 1999), 28.

7. Ideas and products once dismissed as "crazy" include drilling for oil, the telephone, Louis Pasteur's theory of germs, a military use for airplanes, talking movies, quartz time pieces, Federal Express' overnight delivery, and home computing.
8. Martha Lagace, "Lou Gerstner Discusses Changing the Culture at IBM," *HBS Working Knowledge,* December 9, 2002.
9. Buckingham and Coffman, *First Break All the Rules,* 12, 32, 33–36.
10. Ibid., 28.
11. Daniel Goleman, "Leadership That Gets Results," *Harvard Business Review,* March–April 2000, 83.
12. It would be wrong to assume that we don't value such kinds of team-building events. They are often great for having fun together and getting people away from the pressures and routines of the office and into an environment in which they can be more relaxed and open. Special team-building events and activities can supplement ongoing attention to relationships in the group. They just can't replace it.

CHAPTER 4

1. Gerald Olivero, Denise K. Bane, and Richard E. Kopelman. "Executive Coaching as a Transfer of Training Tool: Effects on Productivity in a Public Agency," *Public Personnel Management Journal,* 1997, 26(4), 461–470.
2. For a list of other studies reporting similar conclusions see Andrew W. Talkington, Laurie S.Voss, and Pamela S. Wise, "The Case for Executive Coaching," *Chemistry Business,* November 2002.
3. This paragraph is largely based on the first chapter of John J. Ratey, *A User's Guide to the Brain: Perception, Attention, and the Four Theatres of the Brain* (New York: Knopf Publishing, 2002), 14–47.
4. While highlighting the "plasticity" of the brain—its ability to adapt to its environment—Ratey, nonetheless, acknowledges that there are strong limitations on the extent of this plasticity and that creating new neural connections in adulthood involves immense effort and time.
5. Marcus Buckingham and Donald O. Clifton, *Now, Discover Your Strengths* (New York: Free Press, 2001), 59.
6. David Henry Feldman and Tamir Katzir, "Natural Talents: An Argument for the Extremes," *Behavioral and Brain Sciences,* 1998, 21(3), 414.
7. Françosy Gagné. "A Differentiated Model of Giftedness and Talent," *Gifted,* July 1997, 15–16.
8. Feldman and Katzir, "Natural Talents," 414.

CHAPTER 7

1. Michael S. Malone, "DEC's Final Demise," Forbes.com, Jan. 19, 2001. www.forbes.com/columnists/2001/01/19/0915malone.html.
2. The conclusion of the report evidently stated: "In view of these facts, we feel that Mr. G. G. Hubbard's request for $100,000 for the sale of this patent is utterly unreasonable, since this device is inherently of no use to us. We do not recommend its purchase." As quoted by William von Alven, "Bill's 200-Year Condensed History of Telecommunication." www.cclab.com/billhist.htm.
3. This discussion of the cognitive processes involved in perceiving, as well as the specific terminology "noticing" and "sense-making," relies primarily on William H. Starbuck and Frances J. Milliken, "Executive Perceptual Filters: What They Notice and How They Make Sense," in Donald Hambrick, (Ed.), *The Executive Effect: Concepts and Methods for Studying Top Managers* (Greenwich, Conn.: JAI Press, 1988), 35–65.
4. Starbuck and Milliken, "Executive Perceptual Filters," 39.
5. Joel Barker, "The Business of Paradigms," video (Burnsville, Minn.: Chart-House International Learning Corp., 1989).
6. John Byrne, "CEO Disease," *Business Week,* April 1991, 52–59.
7. John Sherlock, "Learning at the Top," *Journal of Association Leadership,* Summer 2003, 53=54.
8. Jim Collins, "Jim Collins Speaks the Truth," *Journal of Association Leadership,* Summer 2003, 40.
9. Ibid.
10. Starbuck and Milliken, "Executive Perceptual Filters," 48.

CHAPTER 8

1. Ministry of Economic Development and Trade, Government of Ontario, *The Growth Builder's Report: Ontario's Fastest Growing Firms Share Their Insights,* Toronto, 2000, 35.
2. See, for example, "Mergers and Managers Don't Mix." *Management Centre Europe,* Winter 1988. www.mce.be/knowledge/159/37.
3. We do not mean to imply that all technical experts are socially challenged. It has been our experience, however, that there is a general correlation between a strong interest in technology or science and less interest and skill in the social arena. Many individuals are exceptions to this rule, but in the companies we have worked with that have an Expert Orientation, there is usually a corresponding shortage of strong social skills.

4. It would be wrong to push too far the analogy between a civil war and a business context marked by overt and protracted hostility between feuding camps. An actual war obviously inflicts levels of pain, horror, and destructiveness that workplace conflict doesn't match. We certainly don't mean to minimize the horrors of war by using this analogy.

CHAPTER 9

1. If your score indicates a small gap for a Leadership Dimension that you didn't identify as natural to you in Chapter 6, we suggest you reread the descriptions of the Building Blocks for that Dimension in Chapter 3, and then reassess your scores in the assessment at the beginning of this chapter. If you still have a small gap score, then assume that this is a Leadership Dimension that is naturally yours.

CHAPTER 10

1. Edward De Bono, *Lateral Thinking : Creativity Step by Step* (New York: Harper & Row, 1973).
2. An excellent resource for suggestions on how to exercise creative thinking is Roger Von Oech, *A Whack on the Side of the Head* (New York: MJF Books, 1998).
3. Anne Toner Fung, "Reinforcing Change," Adao Institute for Change. www.adao.ca/docs/Reinforcing%20change.pdf.

ABOUT THE AUTHORS

Scott Campbell

Scott Campbell is an internationally recognized speaker and trainer who consults throughout North America with major clients such as Nike, IBM, General Electric, and Proctor & Gamble. His enthusiastic, humorous, and high-energy style, matched by his commitment to thought-provoking, current information and concrete applications, has made him a much-in-demand conference speaker. He has written extensively on the topic of leadership effectiveness for a variety of magazines and journals, and he is the author of *The Quick Guide to the Four Temperaments for Peak Performance.* Campbell is a faculty member with both Type Resources and TRI.

Ellen Samiec

Ellen Samiec is a noted leadership development specialist with international clients that include Xerox, Bio-Lab, and Unisource. The author of *101 Ways to Accomplish More with Less,* she has been featured in the *Globe and Mail, CMA Management,* and the *Financial Post,* and on a variety of radio and television programs. Samiec has more than ten years' experience coaching executives, professionals, and business owners internationally, helping them leverage their strengths to overcome challenges and achieve breakthrough results. She is a certified Master NLP practitioner and trainer with memberships in the Worldwide Association of Business Coaches and the International Coach Federation.

Together Campbell and Samiec are cofounders and directors of 5-D Leadership, a Toronto-based leadership development consulting, training, and coaching consortium.

INDEX

ability: neural networks and, 82; skill vs., 81; storytelling, 84

Abrashoff, Mike, 37–39

acquisitions, 172–173

actions: application of, 47; description of, 47; effectiveness of, 218; implementation of, 47; intention of, 47; vision and, 54

ad hoc leadership, 202–203

alignment of leadership, 138–140

Allard, Kenneth, 227

arbitration, 66

Archimedes Principle: description of, 78–80, 193; example of, 85–88; leadership application of, 80; leveraging your strengths, 80–81; summary of, 88; at work, 82–88

assessments: *BarOn Emotional Quotient Inventory*®, 233; Coaching Building Blocks, 196; Commanding Building Blocks, 195; description of, 70; Enrolling Building Blocks, 196; FIRO-B® instrument, 232; *Leadership Circle Profile*, 234; *Myers-Briggs Type Indicator*® assessment, 231; Relating Building Blocks, 196; Visioning Building Blocks, 195

Bacon, Sir Francis, 194

Bad Data/No Data, 153–156

Barker, Joel, 152

BarOn Emotional Quotient Inventory®, 233

Beals, Vaughan, 27

Beliefs Survey, 122, 129–132

Bennis, Warren, 55, 92

blaming, 157

blended-family context: Leadership Dimensions for, 174–176; mergers and acquisitions, 172–173; Relating in, 175; reorganization, 173; summary of, 188; Visioning in, 175

blind spots, in perceptual filters, 151, 153

Bohr, Neils, 176

brainstorming, 209

bridging of gaps: building the bridge, 208–218; crossing the bridge, 219–220; identifying Building Blocks for, 206–208; knowing your destination, 206–208; leveraging your strengths for, 209–218; overview of, 205–206

Brinkley, Douglas, 9

Buckingham, Marcus, 76, 78

Building Blocks: actions, 47; Coaching. *See* Coaching Building Blocks; Commanding. *See* Commanding Building Blocks; definition of, 47; description of, 75; Enrolling. *See* Enrolling Building Blocks; identification of, 206–208; intention of, 65; Relating. *See* Relating Building Blocks; strengthening of, 199–201; Visioning. *See* Visioning Building Blocks

business contexts. *See* contexts

business rationale for directives, 50

Byrne, John, 154

capacity building, 184

career aspirations and plans, 73

Carlzon, Jan, 30–32

Carnegie, Andrew, 65

Carter, Jimmy: appeals to public by, 8; approval ratings for, 8, 11; beliefs of, 7; Camp David peace accord, 9–10; campaigning by, 7; compromise by, 9; crises during presidency of, 10; factors that helped presidency campaign of, 6–7; Iran hostage crisis, 10–11; leadership approach of, 8–9; loner approach used by, 8–9; persuasion abilities of, 9–10; presidency of, 8; public support lost by, 10; self-reliance of, 8; in Washingtonian politics, 9

Carter Disconnect, 9, 11

Catlin, Katherine, 165

CEO disease, 154–155

Characteristics and Beliefs Checklist, 122–128

civil war context: Commanding in, 183–184; conflict in, 180; description of, 180–181; Leadership Dimensions for, 182–184; Relating in, 183; summary of, 188; Visioning in, 183

classroom-style learning, 76–77

Clifton, Donald O., 76, 78

Coaching: Characteristics and Beliefs Checklist assessment, 127–128; definition of, 40; description of, 25; effective, 74; for expert concentration context, 179; in fast-paced context, 168–169; feedback about, 115; goals of, 69; ineffective, 74; misconceptions regarding, 69; Nestlé example of, 40–42; overview of, 43; in rapid growth context, 166; in smooth sailing context, 187; time investment for, 69; when to use, 43

Coaching Building Blocks: description of, 69; gap assessments, 196; individual career aspirations and plans, 73; individual's strengths, weaknesses, motivations, and potential, 70–71; overview of, 74; performance feedback, 71–72; self-assessments, 196; "stretch" assignments for professional development, 71; teaching and training methods for individual/team learning, 72; team's strengths, weaknesses, motivations, and potential, 70–71

Collins, Jim, 157

command-and-control leadership style, 37, 227–228

Commanding: in blended-family context, 176; Characteristics and Beliefs Checklist assessment, 123, 128; in civil war context, 183–184; contexts for, 48; in crisis, 49; definition of, 26; description of, 25; effective, 52; feedback about, 115; goal of, 48; Harley-Davidson example of, 26–28; ineffective, 52; limitations on use of, 28–29, 34; overuse of, 28–29; overview of, 30; prevalence of, 227–228; staff problems caused by, 29; in sudden crisis context, 171; in urgent situations, 48; when to use, 29–30

Commanding Building Blocks: business rationale for directives, 50; compliance with directives, 51; decision making, 49; description of, 48; directives, 49–50; gap assessments, 195; overview of, 52; priority determination, 49; self-assessments, 195

communication, 187

compelling picture of desirable future, 53–54

competence, 82

conflict mediation, 66–67

Conforti, Silvio, 173

consensus decision making, 60–61, 83

contexts: adapting of, 161; blended-family, 172–176, 188; civil war, 180–184, 188; for Commanding, 48; demands of, 194; distinctiveness of, 161–162; dynamic nature of, 188; expert concentration, 176–180; fast-paced, 166–169, overview of, 189; rapid-growth, 162–166, shifting of, 188; smooth sailing, 184–187; sudden crisis, 169–171

Covey, Stephen R., 112

creative thinking, 209

crisis: leadership in, 2; sudden crisis context, 169–171

Croni, Stephen, 28

de Bono, Edward, 209

Dean, Jimmy, 207

decision making: consensus, 60–61, 83; misperceptions as basis for, 147; perceptions as basis for, 147; top-down, 49

Demille, Nelson, 209

desirable future, 53–54

directives: business rationale for, 50; compliance with, 51; description of, 49–50

effective leadership, 24–25, 43

effectiveness: leadership, 24–25, 43; of leveraging of strengths, 218

Emerson, Ralph Waldo, 122

emotional intelligence, 233

emotional support, 65–66

employee initiative, 55

encouragement, 65–66

Enrolling: Characteristics and Beliefs Checklist assessment, 125, 128; company example of, 34–35; definition of, 33; effective, 62; feedback about, 115; at Harley-Davidson, 34–35; ineffective, 62; overview of, 36; in rapid growth context, 165; in smooth sailing context, 187; when to use, 36

Enrolling Building Blocks: consensus decision making, 60–61, 83; gap assessments, 196; implementing others' worthwhile ideas, 58–59; input from group members, 57–58; overview of, 62; publicly crediting others when their ideas, innovations, or improvements are adopted, 59–60; self-assessments, 196

expert concentration context: Coaching in, 179; description of, 176–177; Leadership Dimensions for, 178–180; Relating in, 179; summary of, 188; Visioning in, 179–180

fast-paced context: Coaching in, 168–169; description of, 166–167; Leadership Dimensions for, 167–169; Relating in, 168; summary of, 188; Visioning in, 168

fear of knowing the truth, 157–158

feedback: Building Block improvements and, 200; definition of, 97; effectiveness evaluated using, 218; in Johari Window, 97–98; performance, 71–72, 200; 360 degree, 112–116

Feldman, David, 81–82

Filter Oblivion: description of, 150–153; strategies for overcoming, 158–159

FIRO-B® instrument, 232

Fishman, Charles, 46

Franklin, Benjamin, 85

Fung, Anne Toner, 219

Gagné, Francoys, 78, 81

gaps: bridging of. See bridging of gaps; description of, 193–194; self-assessment of, 194–198; size of, 197; small. See small gaps

Geldart, Phil, 40–42

genuineness, 57

Gerstner, Lou Jr., 1, 60–61

Giuliani, Rudy, 1, 3–6

Giuliani Moment, 6

Goldsmith, Joan, 55

Goldwyn, Samuel, 154

Goleman, Daniel, 65

Greenstein, Fred, 7

Grimm, Dennis, 70

group dynamics, 175

group members: assessments of, 70–71; encouragement and emotional support of, 65–66; input from, 57–58; valuing of, 63–64; well-being of, 63–64

Harley-Davidson: Commanding at, 26–28; Enrolling at, 34–35

Hoffa, Jimmy, 144

Hussey, Leonard, 16

ideas: evaluation of, 58; implementing of, 58–59; public crediting of, 59–60

imagery, 53

individual: career aspirations and plans of, 73; teaching and training methods for learning, 72; valuing of, 63–64; well-being of, 63–64

initiative, impediments to, 55

innovation, 185

insight, 97–98

instinctive responses, 129, 133–138

interpersonal conflict, 66

James, R. W., 16

Jefferson, Thomas, 122

Jensen, Peter, 53, 68

Johari Window, 94–96

Jung, Carl, 231

Katzir, Tamar, 81–82

Kissinger, Henry, 179

Kotter, John P., 54–55

Kouzes, James M., 25

Laing, R. D., 149

lateral thinking: definition of, 209; development of, 212; examples of, 210, 220; factors associated with, 209; leveraging of strengths using, 210–212; mind-set for, 210 leaders: Bad Data/No Data effects on, 153–156; commitment of followers, 25; desire to please, 154; as heroes, 1–2; openness promoted by, 157; publicly crediting ideas by, 59–60; results-oriented nature of, 24; subordinates' desire to please, 154; trust promoted by, 157; weaknesses of, 19

leadership: ad hoc, 202–203; alignment of, 138–140; approaches to, 2–3; Archimedes Principle applied to, 80; Beliefs Survey, 122, 129–132; command-and-control style of, 37, 227–228; in crisis, 2; effective, 24–25, 43; management vs., 229–230; by others, 84; self-awareness and, 93; successes in, 106–111

Leadership Circle Profile, The, 234

leadership development: action plan for, 224; classroom-style learning, 76–77; self-assessments and, 77; during smooth sailing periods, 185; traditional approaches to, 76–78; weaknesses and, 77–78

Leadership Dimensions: at-a-glance chart of, 132, 139; Beliefs Survey, 122, 129–132; for blended-family context, 174–176; building of, 45–46; Characteristics and Beliefs Checklist, 122–128; for civil war context, 182–184; Coaching. *See* Coaching; Commanding. *See* Commanding; Enrolling. *See* Enrolling; for expert concentration context, 178–180; for fast-paced context, 167–169; identifying of, 119–141; instinctive responses, 129, 133–138; leadership context adapted to, 120; Lego metaphor for, 46; organizational culture that discourages, 121; overview of, 25–26; for rapid growth context, 164–166; Relating. *See* Relating; self-discovery of. *See* self-discovery; for smooth sailing context, 186–187; for sudden crisis context, 170–171; Visioning. *See* Visioning

leadership strengths: checklist for, 100–105; description of, 91–92; feedback about, 112–116; self-awareness of. *See* self-awareness; summary of, 118

learning: classroom-style, 76–77; description of, 56; neural patterns and, 78; strengths as basis for, 82; teaching and training methods for, 72

leverage, 79–80

leveraging of strengths: for bridging of gaps, 209–218; description of, 80–81; to enroll the team, 82–85; example of, 85–88; exercise for, 213–217; keys to, 201; lateral thinking for, 210–212; scenarios for, 213–217, 220–221; for strengthening Building Blocks, 200–201

Lincoln, Abraham, 180

Lipton, Mark, 32

Louis XVI, 144

management: leadership vs., 229–230; in rapid growth context, 163

mediation, 66–67, 183

mentor, 219

mergers and acquisitions, 172–173

military metaphors, 227

misperception: Bad Data/No Data, 153–156; company effects of, 145–146; costs of, 144–145, 149–150; decision making based on, 147; examples of, 145; Filter Oblivion and, 150–153; prevalence of, 156; sources of, 150–156. *See also* perception

modeling, 68

Morgan, J.P., 205

multiple perspectives, 158–159

Myers-Briggs Type Indicator® assessment, 231

natural talent, 81

need for affection, 232

need for control, 232

need for inclusion, 232

neural networks, 82

neural patterns, 78

Nightingale, Earl, 205

noncompliance, 51

noticing, 148–149

organization(s): contexts for. *See* contexts; machine metaphor for, 227–228; mergers and acquisitions, 172–173; military metaphors used by, 227; reorganization of, 173

organizational culture: description of, 121; Leadership Dimensions affected by, 121
O'Toole, James, 2
outside data, 159
Ozley, Lee, 34

Palmer, Arnold, 80
perception: decision making based on, 147; definition of, 148; differences of, 148–149; disagreements about, 146–147; factors that influence, 149; limitations of, 147; recounting of facts based on, 148–149. *See also* misperception
perceptual filters: blind spots in, 151, 153; description of, 143; disadvantages of, 151; Filter Oblivion, 150–153, 158–159; information altered by, 152; information and, 151; misperception. *See* misperception; oblivion of, 150–153; outside data effects on, 159; perspectives used to overcome, 158–159
performance feedback, 71–72, 200
person: valuing of, 63–64; well-being of, 63–64
perspectives, 158–159
Poonjani, Rahim, 146, 148, 151–152
Posner, Barry Z., 25
priorities, 49, 168
productivity, 62

rapid growth context: characteristics of, 163, 188; Coaching in, 166; Enrolling in, 165; Leadership Dimensions for, 164–166; management challenges during, 163; time management during, 165; Visioning in, 165
Reagan, Ronald, 77
reality: misperception of. *See* misperception; strategies to better perceive, 156–159
regression of thinking, 219
Relating: for blended-family context, 175; Characteristics and Beliefs Checklist assessment, 126, 128; for civil war context, 183; definition of, 36; effective, 69; example of, 36–39; for expert concentration context, 179; for fast-paced context, 168; feedback about, 115; goals of, 62; ineffective, 69; overview of, 39; for smooth sailing context, 187; for sudden crisis context, 171; on USS *Benfold*, 36–39; when to use, 39
Relating Building Blocks: caring for well-being of entire person, 63–64; conflict mediation to achieve mutually agreeable resolutions, 66–67; encouragement and emotional support for individual's or group's efforts, 65–66; gap assessments, 196; overview of, 62–63, 69; self-assessments, 196; teambuilding, 67–68
reorganization, 173

Scandinavian Airline Systems, 30–32
seeking new assignments for small gaps, 203–204
self-assessments. *See* assessments
self-awareness: consolidating of, 117; creation of, 100–105; deepening of, 106–111; example of, 99–100; expanding of, 112–117; Johari Window, 94–96; leadership and, 93; valuing of, 92–100
self-discovery: Beliefs Survey, 122, 129–132; Characteristics and Beliefs Checklist, 122–128; false assumptions about, 120; instinctive responses, 129, 133–138
self-knowledge, 94–96, 138
self-unawareness, 93–94
Senge, Peter, 29
sense making, 148–149
September 11, 2001, 3–6
Shackleton, Sir Ernest: crisis management by, 15–18; *Endurance* expedition by, 12–18; leadership skills of, 12–13; personal relationships promoted by, 15; personality qualities of, 12; team unity promoted by, 14–15
Shackleton Secret, 12, 18–19
Sherlock, John, 154–155
skill: ability vs., 81; definition of, 81
Slater, Philip, 92
small gaps: extending your reach for, 201–204; leveraging your strengths for, 200–201; seeking new assignments for closing, 203–204; upping your game for, 198–204

smooth sailing context: Coaching in, 187; description of, 184–185; Enrolling in, 187; Leadership Dimensions for, 186–187; Relating in, 187; summary of, 188; Visioning in, 187

specialization, 203

staff: Commanding approach overuse effects on, 29; "stretch" assignments for professional development, 71

storytelling ability, 84

strengths: of individual, 70–71; Johari Window for identifying, 94–96; leadership. *See* leadership strengths; learning based on, 82; leveraging of. *See* leveraging of strengths; natural, 84–88, 200–201; for synthesis, 84; of team, 70–71

stress, 168–169

"stretch" assignments, 71

sudden crisis context: Commanding in, 171; description of, 169; Leadership Dimensions for, 170–171; Relating in, 171; summary of, 188; Visioning in, 171

talent, 81, 201

team: civil war in, 180; learning in, 72; stages of, 175

teambuilding, 67–68

Teerlink, Richard, 27, 29, 34

thinking: creative, 209; lateral. *See* lateral thinking; regression of, 219

360 degree feedback, 112–116

time management, 87, 165

top-down decision making, 49

Torre, Joe, 40, 65

truth, 157–158

vision: clearing up of, 156–159; communicating of, 54; contribution of

individual and group activities in realizing, 55–56; individual and collective action used to achieve, 54–56; initiative impediments, 55; rapid growth and, 165; setting of, 52–53

Visioning: in blended-family context, 175; Characteristics and Beliefs Checklist assessment, 124, 128; in civil war context, 183; company example of, 30–32; definition of, 30; effective, 56; in expert concentration context, 179–180; in fast-paced context, 168; feedback about, 115; goal of, 52; importance of, 52; ineffective, 56; overview of, 33; power and, 53; for rapid growth context, 165; for smooth sailing context, 187; for sudden crisis context, 171; uses of, 32; when to use, 33

Visioning Building Blocks: communicating of vision, 54; compelling picture of desirable future, 53–54; gap assessments, 195; individual and collective action for achieving vision, 54–55; overview of, 56; recognizing the contribution of individual and group activities in realizing the vision, 55–56; self-assessments, 195

weaknesses: conquering of, 77–78; of individual, 70–71; of leaders, 19; leadership development and, 77–78; strengths created from, 77–78, 83–84; of team, 70–71

Welch, Jack, 1–2

Wheatley, Margaret J., 33

Wilkins, Roger, 10

Wilson, Woodrow, 82

working relationships: description of, 36–37, 63; in fast-paced context, 168